OREGON

COOK BOOK

D1557728

by

Janet Walker

GOLDEN
WEST
PUBLISHERS

Cover — Crater Lake (photo by Dick Dietrich)

Oregon Cook Book Contributors

Anderson, Joanie
Baker St. Bed & Breakfast
Century Farms
Chateaulin Restaurant & Wine Shops
Chetco River Inn
Chick-a-dee Blueberry Nursery
Christie, Ruth
Columbia River Inn Bed & Breakfast
Flora's Lake House Bed & Breakfast
Gillette, Sylvia
Harborside Restaurant
Iris Inn
Lacey's Bomber Inn Restaurant
Lord Bennett's Restaurant & Lounge
Markell, Dorothy
McCarthy, Bob
McCarthy, Kit
Morrison's Rogue River Lodge
Nason, Pearl

Nuzum, Essie
Oak Hill Country Bed & Breakfast
Packwood, Bob (Senator)
Richmond, Bob (Northwest
  Baseball League)
Roberts, Barbara (former Governor)
Romeo Inn Bed & Breakfast
Sanderling Bed & Breakfast
Sea Quest Bed & Breakfast
Smith, Pam
Smith, Verna
Stevens, Lois
Thompson's Bed & Breakfast
Thornton, Al
Thornton, Elsie
Tiegs, Margie (Exec. Dir.
  Rockaway Beach C of C)
Wilkins, Annette
Windward Inn

Thank you!

Printed in the United States of America

5th Printing © 1999

ISBN #1-885590-03-2

Golden West Publishers, Inc.
4113 N. Longview Ave.
Phoenix, AZ 85014, USA
(602) 265-4392

Introduction

Explorers Meriwether Lewis and William Clark made their famous journey to the untouched Oregon Territory in 1805-06. They returned to tell tales of the rich land they had seen, blazing the trail for future westward expansion. To Lewis and Clark, and all those courageous pioneers in oxen-drawn covered wagons who came later, we are thankful for the Oregon we know today.

Oregon attracts more than six million visitors each year! Small wonder!

Oregon is really two different states! On the west side, you can fill your eyes, ears and soul with the sights and sensations of the Pacific Ocean. Visitors can play on the sandy beaches, watch the migrating whales and the playful seals, and explore the oceanside caves.

Here, too, are the majestic towering mountains, deep canyons, rushing streams and the fertile valleys producing bountiful crops of cherries, pears, grapes, berries, asparagus, potatoes and so much more!

Oregon is a majestic state. Consider that dramatic backdrop to Portland, "The City of Roses," awesome 11,235-foot snow-covered Mount Hood, as it peeks out from behind downtown buildings. In Portland, the visitors association reminds visitors that there is no sales tax, no smog, and no streets littered with pop cans.

But, of course, Portland is only the beginning. Within an hour from the state's largest city, you can be clamping on your skis in the mountains, or windsurfing in the Columbia River Gorge, or building sand castles on the beach!

The Willamette River winding through the rolling green hills of the Willamette Valley provides water to grow premium products in Oregon's fertile orchards and vineyards.

The other Oregon on the eastern side features spreading arid sagebrushed plains, rolling wheatlands, highly productive farm-lands, fossil beds and more mountains. One of the most beautiful and deepest lakes in the world, Crater Lake, sits high in the Cascade range.

On the east slopes of the Cascades is Oregon's largest ski area, centered around Bend. It's also whitewater rafting country. To the southeast, scenic desert canyons with spectacular rock formations await discovery. It is a vast, sparsely populated area featuring awesome 30-mile long and 9,670-foot Steens Mountain.

In the northeast part of the state, scenic freeways parallel the historic Oregon Trail, passing through cities with names like Baker City, La Grande and Pendleton. Here you'll discover the beautiful Wallowa and Blue Mountains. Just to the east lies Hells Canyon, the nation's deepest gorge, a mecca for whitewater rafters and anglers.

The recipes presented in this book will provide your palate the opportunity to savor the delicacies for which this glorious state has become famous. You will find highly prized and carefully guarded recipes from some of Oregon's finest eateries and inns, as well as time-honored family favorites.

Come along and join us as we discover the tastes of Oregon!

Table of Contents

Breads

Desserts

Oregon Facts

Population — 3,567,550 (1998)
Area — 97,073 square miles
Highest Elevation — Mt. Hood, 11,235 feet
Lowest Elevation — Sea level, Pacific Ocean
Temperature — High 119, Low -54
Width — (E/W)-345 miles — Length (N/S)-278 miles
Largest City — Portland 458,275; metropolitan area, 1.5 million
Nickname — The Beaver State
State Flower — Oregon Grape
State Tree — Douglas Fir
State Bird — Western Meadowlark
State Animal — Beaver
State Fish — Chinook Salmon
State Gem — Sunstone
Covered bridges:
  - Longest: 'Office Bridge', built 1939, 180 feet across Willamette River
  - Shortest: 'Lost Creek Bridge', built 1919, 39 feet, Jackson County
  - Oldest: 'Upper Drift Creek Bridge', built 1914, Lincoln County

Oregon Tourist Information

Ashland	541-482-3486
Baker Co. C of C	541-523-3356 in-state; 800-523-1235 out-state
Bay-Area C of C	541-269-0215 in-state; 800-824-8486 out-state
Bend Visitor Info	541-382-3221 in-state; 800-905-2363 out-state
Eugene-Springfield	541-484-5307 in-state; 800-547-5445 out-state
Grants Pass	541-476-5510 in-state; 800-547-5927 out-state
Hood River C of C	541-386-2000 in-state; 800-366-3530 out-state
Jacksonville C of C	541-899-8118
Klamath Co.	541-884-0666 in-state; 800-445-6728 out-state
La Grande-Union Co.	541-963-8588 in-state; 800-848-9969 out-state
Lincoln City C of C.	541-994-8378 in-state; 800-452-2151 out-state
Oregon Tourism Div.	541-986-0000 in-state; 800-547-7842 out-state
Pendleton C of C	541-276-7411 in-state; 800-547-8911 out-state
Seaside C of C	503-738-3097 in-state; 888-306-2326 out-state
The Dalles Area	503-623-2564
Tillamook County	503-842-7525

Oregon Web Site: http://www.traveloregon.com

Appetizers

Oregon Razor Clam Fritters

Annette Wilkins — Sherwood

2 cups RAZOR CLAMS, cleaned, chopped, reserve juice
1/4 cup reserved CLAM JUICE
7 Tbsp. FLOUR
1/4 tsp. BAKING SODA
1/2 tsp. SALT
BLACK PEPPER or LEMON PEPPER
5 EGGS, lightly beaten
6 SCALLIONS, including tops, chopped finely
1 tsp. PARSLEY, chopped
2 Tbsp. GREEN PEPPER, chopped fine
1/2 tsp. WORCESTERSHIRE SAUCE

In a medium size bowl, combine all ingredients and mix well. Heat 3 to 4 cups of peanut oil to 360 degrees and drop mixture by spoonful into hot oil, frying until golden brown. Remove with slotted spoon and drain on absorbent paper, repeating until all are done. They are best served immediately, but can be kept warm in a 250 degree oven for 30 minutes. Serve with lemon wedges, tartar sauce or seafood cocktail sauce.

Sunset Cheese Spread

Lee Century Farms — Milton-Freewater

8 oz. CREAM CHEESE
1 (10 oz. tub) SHARP CHEDDAR CHEESE SPREAD
1 Tbsp. OLIVE OIL
1 tsp. GARLIC POWDER
2 Tbsp. BRANDY (optional)
4 to 6 Tbsp. GARLIC HERB WHEATBERRY CAVIAR
2 tsp. GREEN OLIVES, chopped (optional)
2 tsp. CARAWAY SEEDS (optional)
1/2 cup PIMIENTO or GREEN ONIONS (optional)

Warm to room temperature first two ingredients; beat until smooth and combine with remaining ingredients. Cover and chill for up to 6 weeks. Makes 2 3/4 cups.

Since being homesteaded in 1871, five generations of the Lee family have utilized the bountiful Walla Walla Valley land along the Oregon Trail to produce some of the finest farm products grown anywhere.

Smoked Salmon Paté

Chetco River Inn — Brookings

1/4 lb. SMOKED SALMON, skinned, boned
1 (8 oz.) CREAM CHEESE, softened
1/2 tsp. LIQUID SMOKE
2 to 4 drops TABASCO® SAUCE
1 tsp. HORSERADISH
1 Tbsp. LEMON JUICE
2 Tbsp. MAYONNAISE
1 Tbsp. FRESH PARSLEY, minced
2 Tbsp. GREEN ONION BLADES, minced

Combine all ingredients and blend well. Serve with assorted crisp crackers and vegetable pieces, or hot buttered garlic baguette rounds. Makes 2 cups.

Lincoln City Crab Mold

1 can CREAM OF MUSHROOM or CREAM OF CHICKEN SOUP
1 pkg. UNFLAVORED GELATIN, in 3 Tbsp. HOT WATER
2 (3 oz. pkgs.) CREAM CHEESE, softened
1 cup MAYONNAISE
1 cup CELERY, chopped
1 GREEN ONION, finely chopped
1 (7 oz. can) CRAB MEAT, drained, flaked

Heat soup with dissolved gelatin. Blend cream cheese and mayonnaise very well; combine with remaining ingredients, adding soup mixture last. Place in mold, refrigerate overnight and serve with your favorite crackers.

Lincoln City is a seven-mile long community made up of five former smaller cities. Oregon's oldest glass blowing studio is here, as is the world's shortest river, the "D" River. Nearby, built in 1940, Drift Creek covered bridge is the oldest in Oregon.

Curry Dip

Pearl Nason — Klamath Falls

2 cups MAYONNAISE
3 Tbsp. CHILI SAUCE
2 Tbsp. WORCESTERSHIRE SAUCE
1/2 tsp. GARLIC SALT
1 Tbsp. CURRY POWDER, or to taste

Blend all ingredients together and let set overnight in refrigerator. Serve with raw vegetables.

Over 290 days of sunshine a year in Oregon? That's one of the biggest attractions of Klamath Falls, bordered by mountains on one side and semi-arid desert on the other. The city sits atop a subterranean reservoir of high pressure steam which heats schools, homes, businesses and a hospital.

Oven Baked Crab Dip

2 (8 oz. pkgs.) CREAM CHEESE,
  softened
1/3 cup MAYONNAISE
1 Tbsp. POWDERED SUGAR
1 Tbsp. DRY WHITE WINE
1/2 tsp. ONION JUICE
1/2 tsp. PREPARED MUSTARD

1/4 tsp. GARLIC SALT
1/4 tsp. SALT
1 (6 oz. can) CRAB,
  drained, flaked
FRESH PARSLEY,
  chopped
CRACKERS

Combine cream cheese, mayonnaise, powdered sugar, wine, onion juice, mustard and salts; mix well. Gently stir in crab, spoon mixture into lightly greased 1 qt. baking dish. Bake at 375 degrees for 15 minutes. Sprinkle with parsley, serve warm with crackers.

At Gleneden Beach, visitors view an estuary rich in marine life and a sandy beach accented by monolithic rocks.

Crab Dip

2 lg. CREAM CHEESE, softened
1 lb. CRAB
1 lb. CHEDDAR CHEESE, grated
4 HARD BOILED EGGS, chopped
2 Tbsp. DRY MUSTARD
1 jar PIMIENTO, chopped
1/2 cup GREEN PEPPER, chopped
1 cup ONION, diced, sautéed in 1/2 cup BUTTER
SLICED ALMONDS

Mix all ingredients together in pan and stir until all have blended, especially cream cheese. Place in chafing dish, top with sliced almonds and bake at 300 degrees for 15 to 20 minutes. Serve with crackers or spread on small slices of French bread.

Oregon State University in Corvallis is the oldest state supported institution of higher education in Oregon. It was opened in 1858 as Corvallis College.

Stuffed Mushrooms

Joanie Anderson — Beaverton

24 lg. FRESH MUSHROOMS
2 Tbsp. BUTTER
2 Tbsp. ONION, finely chopped
2 tsp. GREEN PEPPER, finely chopped
1/2 cup MILK
FLOUR or CORN STARCH, for thickening
1/4 cup COOKING SHERRY
1/4 tsp. WORCESTERSHIRE SAUCE
dash TABASCO® SAUCE
dash GARLIC POWDER
3/4 cup SHRIMP, fresh or canned

Remove stems from mushrooms; scoop out centers and save. Sauté chopped stems and centers with butter, onion and green pepper. Place mushroom caps in a buttered pan. Make a white sauce of milk, flour, sherry and seasonings, cooking until thick. Combine sautéed mixture with white sauce and shrimp. Spoon over mushroom caps and sprinkle with grated cheese. Bake in 400 degree oven for about 8 minutes, or until bubbling.

Sweet & Sour Chicken Wings

Pearl Nason — Klamath Falls

1 to 1 1/2 lbs. CHICKEN WINGS
GARLIC SALT, to taste
CORN STARCH, for coating
1 EGG, beaten
OIL, for frying
SOY SAUCE

Sauce:
1/4 cup BROTH
1 tsp. SALT
1/4 cup CATSUP
3/4 cup SUGAR
1/4 cup VINEGAR

Remove tips of wings and boil to make broth. Sprinkle wings with garlic salt; roll in corn starch and dip in egg. Fry in shallow cooking oil until brown, sprinkle with soy sauce. Place in baking dish sprayed with vegetable spray. Combine sauce ingredients and heat to boiling. Pour over chicken wings and bake at 350 degrees for 30 minutes. Baste several times. May serve with rice.

Cheese Ball

2 (8 oz. pkgs.) CREAM CHEESE, softened
2 cups SHARP CHEESE, grated
1 Tbsp. PIMIENTO, chopped
1 Tbsp. GREEN PEPPER, chopped
1 Tbsp. ONION, finely chopped
2 tsp. WORCESTERSHIRE SAUCE®
1 tsp. LEMON JUICE
SALT and PEPPER to taste
1 cup PECANS, chopped

Combine all ingredients until thoroughly mixed. Shape into logs or ball, as desired. Roll in chopped pecans. Chill until ready to serve.

Caramel Corn

1/2 cup MARGARINE
1 cup BROWN SUGAR, firmly packed
1/4 cup WHITE CORN SYRUP
1/2 tsp. SALT
1/4 tsp. BAKING SODA
1/2 tsp. VANILLA
3 qts. POPPED CORN
SPANISH NUTS, optional

Melt margarine, stir in brown sugar, corn syrup and salt. Bring to boil and then, without stirring, boil 5 minutes. Remove from heat. Stir in soda and vanilla. Pour over popped corn, mixing well. Turn into 2 large cookie sheets; bake at 250 degrees for one hour, stirring every 15 minutes.

Breakfasts

Deluxe French Toast

4 EGGS
1/4 cup HEAVY CREAM
1/8 cup ORANGE JUICE
1 Tbsp. VANILLA
1 tsp. CINNAMON
1 cup CORN FLAKES, crushed
1/2 cup ALMONDS, slivered
1/4 cup SUGAR
1 Tbsp. CINNAMON
6 slices THICK EGG BREAD
BUTTER, HOT MAPLE FLAVORED SYRUP or JAM

In mixing bowl, whip together eggs, cream, orange juice, vanilla and 1 tsp. cinnamon until blended. Preheat well-greased grill or skillet. In small bowl, mix together corn flake crumbs, almonds, sugar and 1 Tbsp. cinnamon. Turn into shallow pan and set aside. Dip bread quickly into egg batter, and dip into crumb mixture to coat (you may need to spoon some on top and pat into bread.) Cook until golden brown, turn over and cook the other side.

Romeo Inn's Eggs Rarebit

Romeo Inn Bed and Breakfast — Ashland

6 ENGLISH MUFFINS, lightly toasted
6 EGGS, hard cooked, halved
RAREBIT SAUCE
THYME LEAVES (garnish)

Sauce:
  2 Tbsp. BUTTER
  2 Tbsp. FLOUR
  1 cup HALF AND HALF, room temperature
  1/2 cup HENRY WEINHARD'S® DARK BEER, room temperature
  1 cup CHEDDAR CHEESE, grated
  1/2 cup JACK CHEESE, grated
  1 Tbsp. GREY POUPON® MUSTARD
  1/2 tsp. WHITE WORCESTERSHIRE SAUCE
  dash TABASCO®

To prepare the sauce: make a roux of the butter and flour; cook 3 to 4 minutes. Gradually add the warm liquids; bring to a simmer and cook, stirring constantly until mixture thickens. Remove from heat and add remaining ingredients. Stir till cheese melts. To serve, place two muffin halves on a plate; cover with sauce, place an egg half on each sauce-covered muffin; top with a dollop of sauce and garnish with thyme leaves. Serves 6.

Romeo Inn Bed and Breakfast
Built in the early 1930's, this classic elegant Cape Cod house, sits amid gigantic Ponderosa Pines. The snow-capped Siskiyou Mountains provide a backdrop for the charming community of Ashland, famous for its Shakespearean plays. Presented at two indoor theatres from February through October, you can peek behind the scenes on a backstage tour. Be sure to try Lithia spring water which bubbles from the fountains in the park.

Baked Apple French Toast

Oak Hill Country Bed & Breakfast — Ashland

1 lg. loaf (16 oz.) FRENCH BREAD
8 EGGS
3 cups MILK
1 tsp. NUTMEG
1 1/4 Tbsp. VANILLA

3/4 cup SUGAR, divided
5 GRANNY SMITH APPLES
2 Tbsp. CINNAMON
2 Tbsp. BUTTER

Preheat oven to 400 degrees. Spray a 9 x 13 pan with vegetable oil spray, slice bread into 1 1/2 inch slices. Place bread tightly together in one layer in pan. Beat eggs lightly; add milk, nutmeg, vanilla and 1/4 cup sugar. Mix with whisk. Pour half of liquid over bread. Peel, core and slice apples into rings. Place on top of bread to cover. Pour remaining mixture over apples. Mix remaining half cup of sugar with cinnamon and sprinkle evenly over apples. Dot with butter. Bake for 35 minutes. Cool 5 to 10 minutes before serving. Serve with warm maple syrup.

Poached Pears

Oak Hill Country Bed & Breakfast — Ashland

4 to 6 PEARS
1/2 cup MAPLE SYRUP
1/2 cup ORANGE JUICE
peel of ORANGE, cut in strips

Core pears, leaving stem on. Peel and place upright in casserole dish. Pour mixture of syrup, orange juice and peel over pears. Cover and cook in moderate oven until pears are tender.

The towns of Ashland, Medford and Grants Pass are a visitor's first glimpse of Oregon when heading north on I-5. Wolf Creek Tavern, believed to be Oregon's oldest hostelry, is just 20 miles north of Grants Pass. A trip South through the winding pastoral roads of scenic Applegate Valley will bring you to Jacksonville. Many of the buildings have been here since the mid-1850s gold mining boom era.

Whole Wheat Hazelnut Pancakes

Romeo Inn Bed & Breakfast — Ashland

2 EGGS
3/4 cup ALL PURPOSE FLOUR
3/4 cup WHOLE WHEAT FLOUR
1 1/4 cups BUTTERMILK
3 Tbsp. VEGETABLE OIL
2 Tbsp. BROWN SUGAR
1 Tbsp. BAKING POWDER
1/2 tsp. BAKING SODA
1/2 tsp. SALT
1/2 cup TOASTED HAZELNUTS, chopped

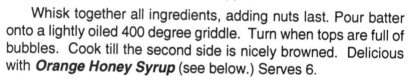

Whisk together all ingredients, adding nuts last. Pour batter onto a lightly oiled 400 degree griddle. Turn when tops are full of bubbles. Cook till the second side is nicely browned. Delicious with *Orange Honey Syrup* (see below.) Serves 6.

More than 90 percent of the nation's hazelnuts come from around McMinnville and Dundee in Yamhill County. Retail outlets offer raw or coated nuts in a variety of flavors. Also known as filberts, these nuts are shipped to buyers worldwide.

Orange Honey Syrup

1 cup HONEY
1/3 cup freshley squeezed ORANGE JUICE
1 Tbsp. BUTTER
1/2 tsp. freshly grated ORANGE PEEL

Combine all ingredients in a small saucepan. Cook, uncovered, over medium heat, stirring frequently, until butter melts and syrup is smooth. Makes about 1 1/4 cups.

Ginger Pancakes with Cinnamon Apples

Sanderling Bed & Breakfast — Yachats

Pancakes:
- 1 1/3 cups FLOUR
- 1 cup WHOLE WHEAT FLOUR
- 1/3 cup POWDERED SUGAR
- 1 1/2 tsdp. BAKING SODA
- 1 tsp. BAKING POWDER
- 1 tsp. CINNAMON
- 1/2 tsp. GINGER
- 1 cup LIGHT SOUR CREAM
- 2 Tbsp. BUTTER, melted
- 1 cup APPLE CIDER or
  APPLE JUICE
- 1/4 cup MILK
- 2 eggs

Topping:
- 1/4 cup BUTTER
- 1 Tbsp. CORN STARCH
- 2 Tbsp. COLD WATER
- 2/3 cup BROWN SUGAR,
  firmly packed
- 1 tsp. CINNAMON
- 3 med. RED APPLES,
  cored, sliced
- 1 cup LIGHT SOUR CREAM
- 2 Tbsp. POWDERED SUGAR
- CINNAMON, for garnish

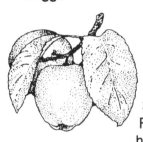

In large bowl, stir together first 7 ingredients. In small bowl, stir together all remaining pancake ingredients until smooth. Stir into flour mixture until well blended. Heat lightly greased griddle to 350 degrees, or until drops of water sizzle. For each pancake, pour 1/4 cup batter on the hot griddle and cook until bubbles form.

Turn pancake and continue cooking 1 to 2 minutes. Keep warm in 200 degree oven until ready to serve. For topping, in 10-inch skillet, melt butter. In small bowl, stir together corn starch and water, adding brown sugar and cinnamon. Stir into melted butter and cook over medium heat, stirring constantly, until sugar dissolves and mixture bubbles and thickens. Stir in apples. Continue stirring constantly, cooking until apples are evenly coated and crisply tender (4 to 7 minutes). In small bowl, stir together sour cream and powdered sugar. Serve apple topping over hot pancakes; dollop with sour cream mixture and sprinkle with cinnamon.

Crispy French Toast

Thompson's Bed & Breakfast — Klamath Falls

4 slices THICK FRENCH BREAD
3 EGGS
3/4 cup MILK
1 tsp. VANILLA
1/4 cup RITZ® CRACKER CRUMBS
1 tsp. CINNAMON
1 Tbsp. BROWN SUGAR
2 Tbsp. BUTTER

Heat buttered grill until hot. Combine eggs, milk and vanilla; dip bread into egg mixture and place on hot grill. Combine remaining ingredients and sprinkle on top of bread slices; turn over and cook until golden brown.

> *Fort Klamath was built in 1863 to protect wagon trains from Indian attacks. This area is one of Oregon's leading cattle producing regions.*

Rice Griddle Cakes

Pam Smith — Bonanza

1 cup RICE, cooked
2 cups MILK, divided
1/2 tsp. SALT
1 Tbsp. SUGAR
1 Tbsp. SHORTENING
1 1/2 cups FLOUR, sifted
2 tsp. BAKING POWDER
1 EGG, beaten

Soak cooked rice in 1 cup of milk overnight in refrigerator. Add salt, sugar, shortening, flour and baking powder; beat mixture well. Add egg and remaining milk. Bake on hot greased griddle. Makes about 20 small cakes. A great way to use leftover rice.

Almond Velvet Freezer Fruit

Baker St. Bed & Breakfast — McMinnville

1 cup PEACHES, peeled, sliced
1/2 cup SUGAR
1 Tbsp. FRUIT FRESH®
1 cup BLUEBERRIES
1 cup STRAWBERRIES, sliced
1 cup RASPBERRIES
1 (8 oz.) ctn. YOGURT
1/2 cup crushed BOXED CEREAL or GRANOLA

Toss peaches, sugar and Fruit Fresh together; then add remainder of fruits. Toss and store in plastic bag in freezer. When ready to serve, allow to thaw for 30 minutes, (or microwave on defrost for 5 minutes). Divide the fruit equally between fruit dishes, champagne glasses, etc. and top with 2 tablespoons yogurt each. Then, top yogurt with 1 tablespoon crushed cereal and serve. A great way to use Oregon's bountiful summer fruits all winter long! Serves 6.

Located in the heart of Oregon's wine country, the **Baker St. Bed & Breakfast** is a 3-story Craftsman style inn featuring a great sitting porch, oriental rugs and loving restoration. In nearby Newberg, a gathering place for boaters and water skiers, the boyhood home of Herbert Hoover is open for tours. A few miles down the road, St. Paul, with a picturesque countryside church built in 1846, hosts one of the oldest and largest rodeos in the Northwest.

Fantastic Spinach Delight

Columbia River Inn Bed & Breakfast — Astoria

1 1/2 cups BISCUIT MIX
1/2 cup MILK
2 EGGS
1 (15 oz. can) SPINACH, drained
1 pt. COTTAGE CHEESE
1 cup CHEDDAR CHEESE, grated
1/2 cup PARMESAN CHEESE, grated
1 tsp. GARLIC GRANULES
4 to 6 EGGS

Stir and mix together biscuit mix, milk and 2 eggs. Spread on bottom of greased, flat 10 x 14 pan. Set aside. In same bowl, place drained spinach, cheeses, garlic and remaining eggs. Spread over first mixture, covering it all. Smooth out and refrigerate overnight. Bake at 350 degrees for 30 to 35 minutes until set. Remove from oven and allow to sit 5 minutes before cutting. Can also be served with additional cheese on top and with biscuits or muffins and fruit. Freezes well before or after baking. Omit garlic, if desired, and substitute 1 cup of chopped green onions.

*Close to the ocean and just blocks from the Columbia River, the **Columbia River Inn Bed & Breakfast** is a beautiful Victorian inn, built in the late 1800's. Astoria was the first permanent European-American settlement in Oregon Country. On the waterfront is the Columbia River Maritime Museum featuring a restored lightship. For an unparalled view, head for the Astoria Column, where a circular 166-step climb will leave you breathless, but amply rewarded. Descendants of fur trader John Jacob Astor are responsible for the Column. Crossing the Columbia at Astoria, the Astoria Bridge is the longest continuous truss span bridge in the world at 4.1 miles.*

Three Pepper Frittata

Oak Hill Country Bed & Breakfast — Ashland

1 SWEET RED PEPPER
1 GREEN PEPPER
1 YELLOW PEPPER
2 Tbsp melted BUTTER
1 tsp. GARLIC POWDER
1 cup CARAWAY SEED JACK CHEESE, grated
1 1/2 cups CHEDDAR CHEESE, grated
12 EGGS
2 cups HALF AND HALF

Cut peppers into strips one inch wide, sauté in butter and garlic powder until heated through. Place in casserole dish and sprinkle on the cheeses. Beat eggs and mix with half and half. Pour over peppers and cheese. Bake until set and brown on top in 350 degree oven.

Oak Hill Country Bed & Breakfast is a charming 1910 farm house inn on the south end of Ashland, offering a large fireplace, an old fashioned front porch and bicycles for tours of the city.

Quickie Quiche

1 can CHEESE SOUP
1 cup MILK
3 EGGS, slightly beaten
1 (8 in. unbaked) PIE SHELL
4 to 6 slices BACON, fried crisp
1 can ONION RINGS

Combine soup with milk and eggs. Crumble bacon into pie shell; sprinkle onion rings on top to taste. Pour soup mixture over all; bake at 375 degrees for one hour or until knife comes out of center clean. Serves 6.

Chile Egg Puff

Oak Hill Country Bed & Breakfast — Ashland

10 EGGS
1/2 cup FLOUR
1 tsp. BAKING POWDER
1/2 tsp. SALT
2 cups COTTAGE CHEESE
4 cups shredded JACK CHEESE
1/2 cup BUTTER or MARGARINE, melted and cooled
2 cans (4 oz.) DICED GREEN CHILES

Preheat oven to 350 degrees. In a medium size bowl, beat eggs until light and lemon colored. Add remaining ingredients, except chiles, blending until smooth. Stir in chiles and pour mixture into a well buttered 9 x 13 inch baking pan. Bake about 35 minutes until top is brown and center appears firm. Serve immediately. Makes 10 to 12 servings.

Amaretto Banana

Oak Hill Country Bed & Breakfast — Ashland

3 BANANAS
VANILLA YOGURT
1 stick BUTTER or MARGARINE
handful of BROWN SUGAR
2 glugs of AMARETTO
CRUSHED ALMONDS

Slice bananas in half, then in half lengthwise. Place one spoonful of yogurt on center of plate, placing bananas on top. Put butter, sugar and amaretto in a glass jar. Place in microwave to melt mixture. Sprinkle crushed almonds over bananas, put one spoonful of amaretto mixture over bananas. Serves 6.

Soups & Chowders

Corn Chowder

2 cups POTATOES, cooked, diced
1 cup CELERY, diced
2 oz. BACON
2 Tbsp. VEGETABLE OIL
1 ONION, diced
3 cups BOILING WATER
1 can CREAM STYLE CORN
1 cup CANNED MILK
SALT and PEPPER to taste
PAPRIKA

Cook potatoes and celery until tender. Meanwhile, chop and fry the bacon; drain well and set aside. Sauté onion in vegetable oil until transparent. Combine boiling water with potatoes, celery and onion; add creamed corn and milk. Heat only to serving temperature. Season to taste; sprinkle servings with bacon and paprika.

Orange Fruit Carrot Soup

Chetco River Inn — Brookings

8 lg. CARROTS
2 med. ONIONS
3 med. POTATOES
1 (48 oz. can) CHICKEN STOCK
2 cups FRESH ORANGE JUICE
1 to 2 Tbsp. ORANGE LIQUEUR, optional
SOUR CREAM
CHIVES

Peal and dice vegetables; add chicken stock and orange juice in a large pot. Cover and cook until tender. Remove from pot and puree; place back in pot. Season with white pepper and salt and orange liqueur, if desired. Serve with dollop of floating sour cream; garnish with chives.

The Oregon Dunes recreation area extends for 40 miles along the coastline north of Brookings. At least 137 different species of birds flock there, including the snowy plover, bald eagle, loons and grebes.

Cabbage Taco Soup

1 to 1 1/2 lbs. GROUND BEEF
1/2 head RED CABBAGE, shredded
1 can RED KIDNEY BEANS
TOMATO JUICE or TOMATO SAUCE
WATER
1 pkg. TACO SEASONING MIX

In large pot, brown beef until no longer red; add cabbage and kidney beans. Now add equal parts tomato juice or sauce and water, and the taco seasoning mix. Cook all day in a crock pot, or simmer an hour or more on stove. Optional ingredients may be added, such as sliced celery, zucchini, etc.

Oregon Coast Clam Chowder

4 slices BACON
1 Tbsp. PAN DRIPPINGS
1 1/2 cups ONION, chopped
1/4 cup FLOUR
1/4 cup CARROT, grated
1/4 cup CELERY, chopped
3 cups POTATOES, peeled, diced
1 tsp. SALT
1/8 tsp. PEPPER
2 (8 oz. cans) CHOPPED CLAMS, drain, reserve liquid
1 cup EVAPORATED MILK

In a large saucepan, cook diced bacon until lightly browned and drain. In reserved drippings, sauté onion until translucent. Stir in flour, add bacon, carrot, celery, potatoes, and seasonings. To reserved clam liquid, add enough water to make 3 cups. Stir into vegetable mixture, bring to boil. Reduce heat and boil gently uncovered 20 minutes, stirring occasionally. Add clams, cook 5 minutes longer. Stir in milk; reheat. Makes 7 1/2 cups.

> *Horseneck clams are abundant in the estuaries of Yaquina Bay, about 100 miles north of Brookings. They are great for clam chowder. However, it was Yaquina Bay oysters that first attracted white settlers in the summer of 1849. Imported Japanese oysters outnumber locals today, but both are fine eating and featured locally in restaurants. In nearby aquariums, you can watch sea otters (rescued from the Alaskan oil spill), sea lions, seals, octopus and tufted puffins.*

New England Clam Chowder

Elsie Thornton — Rockaway Beach

1 pt. SHUCKED CLAMS, drained, reserve liquid
1/3 cup SALT PORK or BACON, diced
1 or 2 med. YELLOW ONIONS, minced
2 cups POTATOES, peeled, diced
1/2 cup WATER
2 cups MILK
1 cup LIGHT CREAM
SALT to taste
1/8 tsp. WHITE PEPPER
1/8 tsp. PAPRIKA

Clean clams for shell fragments; leave whole, mince or grind. Brown pork in heavy saucepan. Add onions and stir fry in drippings 5 to 8 minutes until golden; drain. Add potatoes, water, clam liquid and pork; cover and simmer 10 to 12 minutes until potatoes are nearly tender. Stir occasionally. Add clams, milk, cream, salt and pepper. Cover and simmer 5 minutes to heat through. Do not boil. Ladle into bowls; dust with paprika and serve.

Beer Cheese Soup

Essie Nuzum — Umatilla

3/4 cup BUTTER
1/2 cup CELERY, diced
1/2 cup CARROTS, diced
1/2 cup ONION, diced
1/2 cup FLOUR
1/2 tsp. DRY MUSTARD

1/4 tsp. ACCENT®
2 Tbsp. PARMESAN CHEESE
3 (10 oz. cans) CHICKEN BROTH
6 oz. CHEDDAR CHEESE, grated
1 (12 oz. can) BEER
SALT and PEPPER to taste

In butter, saute vegetables until done but not brown. Blend in flour, mustard, accent, parmesan cheese and chicken broth. Cook 5 minutes, then alternately blend in cheddar cheese and beer. Simmer about 10 minutes before serving.

Tomato Basil Soup

1 lg. ONION, chopped
4 ribs CELERY, chopped
4 cloves GARLIC, minced
1 Tbsp. VEGETABLE OIL
3 qts. CHICKEN BROTH
1 cup TOMATO PASTE
1 cup DRIED BASIL, or to taste
1/2 cup SUGAR
12 to 13 cups CANNED TOMATOES,
    diced, lightly processed in blender
2 cups BUTTER
3 cups FLOUR
4 qts. WHIPPING CREAM

In very large pot or kettle, sauté onion, celery and garlic in oil until tender. Add chicken broth, tomato paste, basil, sugar and tomatoes and simmer 20 minutes. For the roux, in very large saucepan melt butter, whisk in flour and blend in whipping cream. Cook, stirring constantly until mixture is hot and bubbly. Remove from heat and stir in tomato mixture until well blended.

Artichoke Sausage Soup

12 oz. ITALIAN SAUSAGE, sweet or hot
2 (14 oz. cans) ARTICHOKE HEARTS, drained
3 (14 oz. cans) ITALIAN PLUM TOMATOES
1 env. ONION SOUP MIX
3 to 4 cups WATER
1/2 tsp. ITALIAN SEASONING
1/2 tsp. DRIED OREGANO
1/2 tsp. DRIED BASIL

Crumble sausage into pieces in a soup pot (if using link sausage, first remove casing and discard). Brown and drain off fat. Cut artichoke hearts and tomatoes into bite size pieces; add to sausage. Add onion soup mix, water, Italian seasoning, oregano and basil; heat through.

Bouillabaisse

Al Thornton — Rockaway Beach
"Makes a good meal with garlic bread and green salad."

1/2 cup OLIVE OIL
1 med. ONION, chopped
2 med. CARROTS, scraped, chopped
2 med. CELERY RIBS, chopped
2 (14 1/2 oz. cans) PEELED DICED TOMATOES in own juice
2 cups DRY WHITE WINE
4 (10 oz. cans) CLAM JUICE
1 Tbsp. GARLIC POWDER
1/4 cup DRIED BASIL
1 1/2 tsp. GROUND PEPPER
1 1/2 tsp. TABASCO® SAUCE
SALT optional
12 FRESH CLAMS, cleaned
12 FRESH MUSSELS, debearded, (cleaned)
1/2 lb. LARGE UNCOOOKED SHRIMP, peeled, deveined
1 lb. RED SNAPPER FILLETS, cut into large chunks
1 lb. SALMON FILLETS, cut into large chunks
1 lb. SCALLOPS

(Note: To clean clams and mussels; scrub well. Cover with cool water, to which 1 Tbsp. salt has been added. Let stand for 30 minutes. Rinse in cold water and drain. Only eat clams and mussels that have opened when cooked.)

In a 6 qt. kettle or Dutch oven, heat oil over medium heat and saute onion, carrot and celery until onion is translucent. Add tomatoes, wine, clam juice and spices and bring slowly to a boil. Reduce heat and simmer until vegetables are tender, about 5 minutes. Add all fish; increase heat to medium-low. Cook covered 8 to 10 minutes until clams and mussels open, and other fish flakes easily. Remove fish with slotted spoon to warm platter. Taste the broth and salt if necessary, serve in soup bowls.

> *In Charleston, deep sea fishing is a way of life. Many species are abundant in the Pacific Ocean waters. Crabbing and clamming are popular recreational activities.*

Salads

Curried Rice Crab Salad in Tomato Rosettes

Annette Wilkins — Sherwood

1/2 lb. CRAB MEAT
1 1/4 cups COOKED RICE, chilled
1/2 cup CELERY, chopped
2 GREEN ONIONS, chopped
1/4 cup SLICED WATER CHESTNUTS
1 Tbsp. LEMON JUICE
1/2 tsp. SOY SAUCE

1/4 tsp. SALT
dash PEPPER
1/2 tsp. CURRY POWDER
1/2 cup MAYONNAISE
6 med. TOMATOES
LETTUCE LEAVES
PAPRIKA to garnish

Combine crab, rice, celery, onions and water chestnuts. Mix lemon juice and seasonings with mayonnaise and add to crab mixture. Toss to coat lightly. With stem end down, cut tomatoes into six wedges being careful not to cut them clear through the base. Spread sections apart. Sprinkle with salt and pepper. To serve, place tomato on lettuce lined plates and fill with crab-rice mixture. Garnish with paprika.

Oregon Raspberries & Cream Salad

1 (3 oz. pkg.) LEMON FLAVORED GELATIN
2 cups BOILING WATER
4 cups MINIATURE MARSHMALLOWS
1 (3 oz. pkg.) RASPBERRY GELATIN
1 1/3 cups BOILING WATER
1 (10 oz. pkg.) FROZEN OREGON RASPBERRIES
1 (8 oz. pkg.) CREAM CHEESE, softened
1 cup HEAVY CREAM
1 (8 oz. can) CRUSHED PINEAPPLE, undrained

In large bowl, stir lemon gelatin and boiling water until gelatin is completely dissolved. Stir in marshmallows and set aside. In medium bowl, stir raspberry gelatin and boiling water until gelatin is completely dissolved. Add frozen raspberries; stir until thawed. Pour into 8 cup mold. Refrigerate until set but not firm, about 20 to 30 minutes. In small bowl, using mixer at medium speed, beat cream cheese until smooth. Gradually beat in heavy cream; continue beating until thick and fluffy. Set aside. Place bowl of lemon gelatin in large bowl of ice cubes and water. Stir until gelatin mixture is slightly thickened; stir in undrained pineapple. Fold in cream cheese mixture; spoon over raspberry layer and cover. Refrigerate until firm; unmold onto serving plate. Serves 16.

Woodburn bills itself as the "World's Berry Center". All kinds of berries proliferate here, namely blackberries, strawberries, gooseberries, raspberries and currants. The Santiam blackberry is a real favorite for pies, jams and syrups.

Broccoli Gourmet Salad

Lacey's Bomber Inn Restaurant — Milwaukie

1 head BROCCOLI FLORETS, cut small
1/2 lb. TOASTED ALMONDS, sliced
1/2 lb. BACON, fried crisp, diced
1/4 cup GREEN ONIONS, sliced
1/2 cup CELERY, sliced
1/2 lb. GREEN GRAPES, cut in half

Dressing:
1 cup RAISINS
1 cup MAYONNAISE
1 Tbsp. VINEGAR
1/3 cup SUGAR

Combine salad ingredients. Mix together dressing ingredients, stirring to dissolve sugar. Combine salad and dressing and let stand 3 to 4 hours before serving.

Art Lacey purchased a retired bomber airplane from the U. S. Air Force, flew it from Oklahoma to Milwaukie, Oregon, and a year later (in 1948), opened a restaurant. Today, **Lacey's Bomber Inn Restaurant,** *currently operated by his daughter, Punky Scott, still serves selections with titles like, "G. I. Joe", "Fly-by", "Tokyo Rose" and "Sentimental Journey".*

Ice Box Salad

28 lg. MARSHMALLOWS, cut into thirds
1 (8 oz. can) CRUSHED PINEAPPLE, and juice
1/2 pt. WHIPPING CREAM
1/2 cup NUTS, chopped
8 oz. MARASCHINO CHERRIES, drained

Mix marshmallows and pineapple together and refrigerate 24 hours. Just before serving, whip cream, combine with nuts and cherries (cut in half). Combine with marshmallow mixture; decorate with additional cherries and nut meats.

Tangy Waldorf Salad

2 cups TART APPLES, cubed
2 cups CELERY, diced
1 cup RAISINS
1 cup WALNUT HALVES

In large bowl, combine all ingredients. Toss with dressing, below. Serve on bed of lettuce.

Dressing:
1/3 cup OIL
3 Tbsp. RED WINE VINEGAR
3 Tbsp. APPLE JUICE CONCENTRATE, frozen, thawed
3/4 tsp. DILL WEED
SALT and PEPPER to taste
1 cup BLUE CHEESE or FETA CHEESE, crumbled

In small bowl, whisk together all ingredients, except cheese. When well combined, stir in cheese.

In addition to tasting super-delicious, apples are a virtual fiber factory. Each apple has as much fiber as a bowl of cold cereal. Fiber (apple pectin) helps to lower your blood cholesterol and apples have no cholesterol. Apples are very low in sodium. They have less sodium than ordinary tap water. They contain niacin, calcium, iron, potassium, phosphorous, vitamins A, B, B2 and C, and boron to help prevent osteoporosis.

High Desert Chicken Salad

1 1/2 cups CHICKEN, cooked, chopped
1 cup PINEAPPLE TIDBITS
1 cup APPLE, chopped
3/4 cup GRAPES, cut in half
1/2 cup PECANS, chopped
1/2 cup RAISINS
1/2 cup MAYONNAISE
CURRY POWDER to taste

Combine all ingredients, except last two. Mix mayonnaise and curry, and then combine with salad ingredients. Chill.

Apple Salad

6 DELICIOUS APPLES, chopped, unpeeled
1 1/2 cups CELERY, diced

Dressing:
    3/4 cup SUGAR
    1 EGG, beaten
    3 Tbsp. WATER
    1 1/2 tsp. VINEGAR
    2 Tbsp. MARGARINE

Combine sugar, egg and water, then add vinegar and margarine, blending well. Cook in double boiler until thick. May thin, if necessary, with milk or mayonnaise. Pour over apples and celery; store in refrigerator.

Orange Sherbet Salad

1 (6 oz. pkg.) ORANGE FLAVORED GELATIN
2 cups BOILING WATER
2 (11 oz. cans) MANDARIN ORANGES, drained, reserving liquid
1 pt. ORANGE SHERBET, softened slightly
1 cup DAIRY SOUR CREAM
1 (20 oz. can) PINEAPPLE CHUNKS, drained
1 (16 oz. can) FRUIT COCKTAIL, drained

Into large mixing bowl, pour gelatin powder and add boiling water, stirring until dissolved. When gelatin starts to cool, add sherbet, the juice from the mandarin oranges and sour cream. Pour entire mixture into blender container. Secure lid and blend for a minute or so. Pour mixture back into mixing bowl and add well-drained fruits. Pour salad into a mold and serve on lettuce-lined plates. Serves 10 to 12.

Cranberry Salad

2 (1 lb. cans) CRANBERRY SAUCE
2 env. PLAIN UNFLAVORED GELATIN
1/2 cup COLD WATER
2 cans MANDARIN ORANGES, drained
1 (3 oz. pkg.) CHOPPED NUTS

Crush cranberry sauce with fork; heat in top of double boiler until dissolved. Soften gelatin in cold water, add to hot cranberry sauce and stir till dissolved. Add oranges and nuts. Pour into mold and chill until firm.

Axe throwing, tree topping, tree climbing, log rolling and log chopping may not be your cup of tea, but in Albany, near Portland, they attract contestants from around the world each July. One of the nation's largest Veterans' Day parades is in Albany, which boasts some of the world's largest rye grass seed and mint crops.

Mint

Quick 'n Easy Chicken Salad

1 cup DAIRY SOUR CREAM
1 pkg. INSTANT ONION SOUP MIX
2 cups CHICKEN, cooked, cubed
2 cups BROCCOLI FLORETS, cooked
1 cup WALNUTS or PECANS, chopped

Combine sour cream and dry soup, mixing well. Combine chicken, broccoli, and nuts; mix well. Stir into sour cream mixture, chill covered 1 to 2 hours to allow flavors to develop. Serves 4.

Shrimp Macaroni Salad

1 (8 oz. pkg.) SMALL SHELL MACARONI
DILL WEED
2 ribs CELERY, finely chopped
2 or 3 HARD BOILED EGGS
1 lg. DILL PICKLE, finely chopped
1 cup GREEN ONION, diced
12 OLIVES, sliced
2 tsp. PREPARED MUSTARD
1 Tbsp. LEMON JUICE
1/2 cup each MAYONNAISE, SOUR CREAM, TARTAR SAUCE
1 lb. SHRIMP, cooked

Boil macaroni per package directions; rinse, add dill weed and chill. Add celery, chopped eggs, pickle, green onion and olives. Mix mustard, lemon juice, mayonnaise, sour cream and tartar sauce into above mixture. Add shrimp last; best if chilled overnight.

Pizza Salad

Salad:
   1/2 lb. BULK or ITALIAN LINK SAUSAGE
   1 head LETTUCE
   1 cup JACK CHEESE, cut in strips
   1 1/2 cups RIPE OLIVES
   1 cup CHERRY TOMATOES, cut in half
   1 1/2 cups GARLIC CROUTONS
Dressing:
   1/2 cup SALAD OIL
   6 Tbsp. VINEGAR
   2 Tbsp. SUGAR
   2 tsp. OREGANO
   1/2 tsp. GARLIC SALT

Crumble sausage and sauté over high heat until cooked. Drain. Tear lettuce into salad bowl, top with cheese strips, cooked sausage, olives, tomatoes and croutons. Toss with dressing and serve. Serves 4.

Zippy, Zingy Seven-Up Salad

Salad:
- 1 lg. LEMON GELATIN
- 2 cups BOILING WATER
- 2 cups 7-Up®, SPRITE® or FRESCA®
- 1 (20 oz. can) CRUSHED PINEAPPLE, drained, reserve liquid
- 3 BANANAS, chopped
- 2 cups MINIATURE MARSHMALLOWS

Topping:
- 1/4 cup SUGAR
- 2 Tbsp. FLOUR
- 1 cup LIQUID (reserved juice plus water)
- 1/2 to 3/4 tsp. LEMON JUICE
- 1 EGG, beaten
- 2 Tbsp. BUTTER
- 1 (8 oz. pkg.) CREAM CHEESE, softened

Dissolve lemon gelatin in boiling water; add soda. When slightly thickened, add well-drained pineapple, bananas and miniature marshmallows. Place in 9 x 13 pan and refrigerate until well set. Meanwhile, mix sugar with flour, adding liquid, lemon juice and egg; cook until very thick. Cool slightly and add butter and cream cheese; frost the gelatin and return to refrigerator.

Chicken Macaroni Salad

- 1 pt. SOUR CREAM
- 1 pkg. KNORR® VEGETABLE SOUP MIX
- 1/2 to 3/4 cup SALAD DRESSING
- 1 (7 oz. pkg.) ELBOW MACARONI, cooked, drained, chilled
- 3 to 4 cups CHICKEN, cooked, cubed, chilled
- SALT to taste

In a large bowl, combine sour cream and dry soup mix, mixing thoroughly. Cover and chill overnight. Stir in salad dressing, macaroni, chicken and salt. Blend lightly, but thoroughly. Cover and chill 3 or more hours before serving. Serves 8.

Orange Apricot Gelatin

Salad:
- **2 sm. pkgs. ORANGE GELATIN**
- **2 cups BOILING WATER**
- **1 cup PINEAPPLE JUICE**
- **1 cup APRICOT JUICE**
- **1 lg. can CRUSHED PINEAPPLE, drained & mashed**
- **1 lg. can APRICOTS, drained**
- **1 cup MINIATURE MARSHMALLOWS**

Frosting:
- **1 cup PINEAPPLE JUICE**
- **1 cup APRICOT JUICE**
- **1/2 cup SUGAR**
- **2 Tbsp. FLOUR**
- **1 EGG, beaten**
- **2 Tbsp. BUTTER**
- **1 cup WHIPPING CREAM, whipped**
- **GRATED CHEESE, optional**

Combine gelatin and boiling water and add juices. Add in pineapple, mashed apricots and marshmallows. Place in 9 x 13 pan; refrigerate until firm. For frosting, heat juices in saucepan, add combined sugar and flour. Stir until well mixed; add egg and butter. Cook until thick; cool. Add whipped cream and spread over firm gelatin. Top with grated cheese.

Think of it—a small country store that has been serving customers since 1890. Almost sounds impossible—but you will find one in Winston-Dillard, where you can also watch lions, tigers and elephants safely from your car as they roam freely in a 600-acre reserve.

Spinach Salad

Dressing:
- **1 cup OIL**
- **1/2 cup SUGAR**
- **1/2 cup CATSUP**
- **1/4 tsp. WORCESTERSHIRE SAUCE**
- **1 med. ONION, grated**

Salad:
- **20 oz. FRESH SPINACH**
- **1 1/2 cups BEAN SPROUTS**
- **1 can SLICED WATER CHESTNUTS**
- **6 slices BACON, cooked, crumbled**
- **6 HARD COOKED EGGS, peeled and chopped**

Prepare dressing. Combine all ingredients, stirring to dissolve sugar. Four hours prior to serving, wash and drain spinach. In a large bowl, place drained bean sprouts, water chestnuts, bacon and spinach. Pour half the dressing over salad ingredients. DO NOT TOSS. Chill four hours. Then add remaining dressing and toss. Sprinkle with egg and serve immediately.

Shrimp Salad

- **4 cans SMALL SHRIMP, drained**
- **1 cup CELERY, diced**
- **1 cup GREEN ONIONS, diced**
- **1/3 cup GREEN PEPPER, diced**
- **1/4 cup PIMIENTO, diced**
- **2 cups BLACK OLIVES, sliced**
- **2 cups MAYONNAISE**
- **1/4 cup HEAVY CREAM**
- **1/4 cup VINEGAR**
- **1 can CHINESE NOODLES**

In a large bowl, combine first 6 ingredients. In small bowl, mix together mayonnaise, cream and vinegar; add to shrimp mixture. Blend lightly but thoroughly. Cover and chill overnight. Just before serving, stir in noodles.

Oriental Pea Salad

2 strips BACON
1 1/2 tsp. BACON DRIPPINGS
1/4 cup MAYONNAISE
2 Tbsp. SOUR CREAM
1/4 tsp. SALT
1/2 tsp. WHITE PEPPER

2 (10 oz. pkgs.) FROZEN
   PEAS, thawed
2 oz. ORIENTAL PEA PODS
1/4 cup RED ONION, diced
2 oz. SLICED WATER
   CHESTNUTS

Cut bacon into 1/4 inch pieces and spread evenly in small baking pan, bake at 350 degrees until evenly cooked (about 10 minutes) stirring frequently. Drain, reserving 1 1/2 tsp. drippings. Refrigerate bacon, let drippings cool to room temperature. In a small bowl, combine mayonnaise, sour cream, salt and pepper; stir in reserved bacon drippings and bacon, mixing well. Set aside. To assemble salad, turn peas, pea pods, onion, and water chestnuts into salad bowl. Add mayonnaise mixture and mix in gently. Serves 10 to 12.

In central Oregon, Madras enjoys the distinction of being Oregon's major potato producing area. Madras is surrounded by high arid desert terrain and jagged mountain peaks.

Sour Cream Potato Salad

6 cups POTATOES
1/4 cup GREEN ONION,
   chopped with tops
1 tsp. CELERY SEED
1 1/2 tsp. SALT
1/2 tsp. PEPPER

4 HARD COOKED EGGS
1 cup SOUR CREAM
1/2 cup MAYONNAISE
1/4 cup VINEGAR, or less,
   to taste
1 tsp. PREPARED MUSTARD

Boil potatoes in skins, cool and dice. Combine potatoes, onions, celery seed, salt and pepper, toss lightly. Separate whites from yolks, chop whites and add to potato mixture; chill. Mash yolks, add sour cream, mayonnaise, vinegar and mustard, mix well. Pour over potatoes, toss lightly and chill.

Cherry Gelatin Salad

1 can CHERRY PIE FILLING
1/2 cup SUGAR
1 (20 oz. can) CRUSHED PINEAPPLE
1 lg. box CHERRY GELATIN
juice of 2 ORANGES
juice of 1 LEMON

Mix first 3 ingredients in a pan, bring to boil. Remove from heat; add dry gelatin. Mix in juices, place mixture into mold or flat casserole container. Chill until firm.

Lakeview has been called "Oregon's Tallest Town", because of its 4,800 foot elevation. This former ghost town now has all the trimmings, and Western hospitality is commonplace. Nearby, Old Perpetual, the state's only continuously spouting geyser, shoots 200 degree water 60 feet into the air. Explore Christmas Valley and its high desert country filled with lava flows, cinder cones and a lost forest.

Molded Crab or Shrimp Salad

Lois Stevens — Rockaway Beach

1 pkg. LEMON GELATIN
1 1/2 cups WATER, boiling
1 Tbsp. VINEGAR
pinch SALT
1/2 cup CATSUP WITH CHILI PEPPER or, 1 can TOMATO ASPIC
1 sm. ONION, grated
1/2 cup CELERY, chopped
1 cup CRAB or SHRIMP

Combine gelatin with water, cool slightly. Add remaining ingredients; pour into dish or mold. Refrigerate until set.

Chicken & Grapes Salad

5 1/2 cups CHICKEN, chopped, cooked
3 HARD BOILED EGGS, chopped
1 cup CELERY, diced
1 cup SWEET PICKLES, diced
1 cup PECANS, toasted, chopped
1/2 cup GREEN GRAPES, cut in half
1/2 cup RED GRAPES, cut in half
1 (8 oz. can) SLICED WATER CHESTNUTS
1 (8 oz. can) PINEAPPLE TIDBITS, drained
1/2 cup STUFFED GREEN OLIVES
1 sm. ONION, finely chopped
1 (2 oz. can) PIMIENTO
1 Tbsp. LEMON JUICE
1 cup MAYONNAISE

Combine all ingredients, blending well. Chill. Serve on bed of lettuce. Serves 12.

Seven miles south of Bend, it's fun to try to make eye contact with the Great Horned Owl or to find the lizards hiding in their display at the High Desert Museum. A bit further south you can stand at the base of Lava Butte, a 500-foot cinder cone.

Tailgate Salad

Lee Century Farms — Milton-Freewater

1/2 (8 1/2 oz. jar) GARLIC HERB FLAVOR WHEATBERRY CAVIAR
1 (16 oz. can) BLACK BEANS, rinsed, drained
4 oz. JACK CHEESE, cut into 1/4 inch cubes
1 (8 oz. can) WHOLE KERNEL CORN, drained
3/4 cup GREEN ONIONS, with tops, sliced
3/4 cup CELERY, thinly sliced
1 sm. RED BELL PEPPER, diced
2 Tbsp. OLIVE OIL
2 Tbsp. LEMON JUICE
1 clove GARLIC, minced

Mix all ingredients, tossing lightly; chill. Stir before serving. May be made 24 hours before serving. Serves 6 or 8.

Fruit Salad with Cooked Dressing

Joanie Anderson — Beaverton

3 lg. CRISP APPLES, cut up
3 lg. BANANAS, cut up
1 lg. can CHUNK PINEAPPLE
**   drain, reserve juice**
WHITE GRAPES, if desired

Dressing:
**   1 cup reserved PINEAPPLE JUICE**
**   2 EGGS, beaten**
**   1 1/2 Tbsp. FLOUR**
**   juice of 2 LEMONS**
**   1 Tbsp. BUTTER**

Prepare fruit and place in large serving bowl arranging apples and pineapple first. Gently layer fruits in bowl. Cook all remaining ingredients in double boiler until thick. Cool to lukewarm. Pour over fruit. Tastes like a lemon pie.

> *Beaverton was appropriately named for the abundance of beaver dams in the area in 1868. Today, more than 300 acres of vineyards, some offering tours, complement the surrounding farm lands.*

Homemade French Dressing

Annette Wilkins — Sherwood

When there is about 1 1/2 inches of **catsup** left in the bottle, add about 1 1/2 inches of **oil**, 2 inches of **vinegar, salt, pepper, garlic powder** and perhaps **cloves**, and 1/2 tsp. **sugar**. Close bottle and shake well to mix; add 1/2 pkg. **fruit pectin**. Again shake well and return to refrigerator.

Main Dishes

Harborside Ostrich

Harborside Restaurant — Portland

5 oz. OSTRICH THIGH MEAT	**MUSHROOMS, sliced**
FLOUR	**SUN-DRIED TOMATOES**
CANOLA OIL	**RED WINE**
GARLIC, chopped finely	**BROWN GRAVY**

Tenderize the ostrich meat. Dredge in flour, then sauté in canola oil. Drain excess oil, and add remaining ingredients (to taste). Return pan to heat for about 30 seconds, and deglaze with red wine. Add brown gravy (demi-glaze) which you may prepare yourself or buy. Reduce heat, and cook to desired sauce consistency.

Ostriches are raised throughout Oregon. One large breeding farm (270 acres) is located on Sauvie Island. Properly prepared, it is tender, tastier and lower in fat and calories than beef or chicken. You may prepare ostrich in the same manner that you would prepare pork tenderloin.

Butterflied Leg of Lamb

Morrison's Rogue River Lodge — Merlin

1 (4 or 5 lb.) boned and butterflied LEG OF LAMB
1/2 cup OLIVE OIL
1 clove minced GARLIC
1/2 tsp SALT
1/2 tsp. PEPPER
1 Tbsp. concentrated ORANGE JUICE
1/2 cup FRESH HERBS, (BASIL, ROSEMARY, THYME, etc.)

Place prepared meat in container to marinate. (You must trim every bit of fat from the meat first.) Blend together all remaining ingredients. Pour over lamb. After marinating, barbecue over medium hot coals 20 to 30 minutes or until internal temperature is 140 degrees. Let set 20 minutes before cutting. Serve with mint jelly, or **Apple Pear Chutney** (see below).

Morrison's Rogue River Lodge was built in 1946 by a fishing guide, Lodge Morrison. It has become a haven for rafters all summer and fishermen in the fall. Spring and fall runs of chinook salmon and steelhead trout lure many serious anglers.

Apple Pear Chutney

Morrison's Rogue River Lodge — Merlin

2 qts. APPLES, peeled, chopped
4 cups BROWN SUGAR
1 qt. CIDER VINEGAR
1 clove GARLIC, minced
1 ONION, chopped
3 med. RED PEPPERS, chopped
1 Tbsp. SALT

1 pod HOT PEPPER
1 lb. RAISINS
2 Tbsp. MUSTARD SEED
1 whole ORANGE, diced
2 Tbsp. GROUND GINGER
2 qts. PEARS, peeled and chopped

Simmer first 6 ingredients until fruit is tender. Add next 6 ingredients and continue simmering 30 minutes more. Add pears and let set covered overnight. Do not cook. In the morning, bring the mixture to a boil and pour into hot sterile jars. Seal and store in a dark, cool place. Also delicious with fresh pork or ham.

Country Fried Pork Chops

4 PORK CHOPS
1 (2 oz. can) SLICED
   MUSHROOMS, drained
1 can CREAM OF CELERY SOUP

1/2 cup WATER
1/4 tsp. THYME, crushed
6 sm. WHOLE WHITE ONIONS
1 cup CARROTS, sliced

In skillet, brown chops and mushrooms in shortening. Pour off fat, then stir in soup, water and thyme. Add onions and carrots. Cover and cook over low heat for 45 minutes, or until tender.

Wild Rice Stew

1 1/2 lbs. BEEF STEW MEAT
RED WINE, optional
1 pkg. UNCLE BENS® LONG GRAIN AND WILD RICE,
   including seasoning
1 can ONION SOUP, undiluted
1 can CREAM OF MUSHROOM SOUP, undiluted

Marinate meat in wine, if desired. Mix all ingredients in casserole dish. Bake in 325 degree oven, covered, for about 2 hours.

Veal Parmigiana

2 Tbsp. BUTTER
1 lb. FROZEN BREADED VEAL PATTIES
1 (15 1/2 oz. jar) SPAGHETTI SAUCE
1 cup MOZZARELLA CHEESE, grated
2 Tbsp. PARMESAN CHEESE
PARSLEY, for garnish

In a large skillet, heat butter over medium heat. Brown patties until golden, about 3 minutes per side. Remove to heated plate. Wipe out skillet. In same skillet, heat spaghetti sauce until bubbly; arrange patties on sauce. Sprinkle with cheeses; cover and cook over medium heat 10 minutes. Serve with cooked pasta and additional grated parmesan. Garnish with parsley. Serves 4.

Hazelnut Stuffed Chicken Breast

Chateaulin Restaurant — Ashland

1/2 lb. CREAM CHEESE
1/2 cup roasted HAZELNUTS, skinned, coarsely chopped
2 SCALLIONS, minced
8 fresh CHICKEN BREASTS (4 oz. ea.), boneless, skinless
2 oz. UNSALTED BUTTER
SALT and WHITE PEPPER to taste

Preheat oven to 400 degrees. In a small mixing bowl, blend cream cheese, nuts and scallions. With the tip of a sharp boning knife, cut a small pocket lengthwise in the side of each chicken breast. Divide cream cheese mixture evenly and press into pockets of chicken breasts. Melt butter and brush the bottom of a baking dish and the tops of the chicken breasts. Season breasts lightly with salt and pepper. Place breasts in baking dish in single layer. Cover with lid or foil and bake 12 minutes. Turn breasts and cook about 8 to 10 minutes more until done. Serve with *Champagne Sauce* (see below).

Champagne Sauce

6 oz. DRY SPARKLING WINE or CHAMPAGNE
6 oz. DEMI-GLAZE (reduced brown stock)
2 Tbsp. SHALLOTS, chopped
1 LEMON, juiced
3 oz. HEAVY CREAM
4 oz. UNSALTED BUTTER

In a small saucepan combine champagne, demi-glaze, shallots and lemon juice and reduce over high heat until only about one half remains. Add cream and reduce the liquid volume again by half. Reduce heat and gently whisk in butter in small pieces until fully incorporated. Place breasts on a serving platter and top with champagne sauce. Garnish with toasted **hazelnuts, parsley sprigs** and **lemon wedges.** An elegant dinner entree for special guests that is easy to prepare ahead of time.

Porcupine Meatballs

1 lb. GROUND BEEF
1/2 cup BREAD CRUMBS
1 EGG
1 tsp. WORCESTERSHIRE SAUCE
3/4 tsp. SALT
1 Tbsp. PARSLEY FLAKES

1 Tbsp. ONION, minced
1/3 cup UNCOOKED RICE
1 (8 oz. can) TOMATO
  SAUCE
1/2 tsp. SEASONING SALT
1 cup WATER

Combine beef, crumbs, egg, Worcestershire, salt, parsley and onions. Mix and shape into 8 meatballs. Roll each ball in the rice so that it adheres. Place meatballs in a skillet, combine tomato sauce and seasoning salt; pour over each meatball. Carefully pour the water into the skillet around and in between the meatballs, not over them. Cover skillet with lid and simmer over medium heat for about 45 minutes.

Pioneer Meatballs

1 lb. GROUND BEEF
2 EGGS, beaten
1/3 cup TOMATO JUICE
1 cup OATS
2 Tbsp. ONION, grated
1 tsp. PARSLEY

1 tsp. SALT
dash PEPPER
1/8 tsp. NUTMEG
1 can MUSHROOM SOUP
1/2 cup BUTTERMILK

Combine all ingredients, except soup and buttermilk. Shape into balls and brown in heavy skillet. Combine soup and buttermilk; pour over meatballs. Cover and bake at 300 degrees for one hour. Serves 4.

Before venturing on the Oregon Trail, pioneers were advised to take 200 pounds of flour, 150 pounds of bacon, 10 pounds of coffee, 20 pounds of sugar, and 10 pounds of salt for provisions. In addition, they would need a baking kettle, coffee pot, tin plates and cups.

Elegant Chicken Casserole

6 CHICKEN BREASTS
WATER
1 (10 oz. pkg.) CHOPPED BROCCOLI, thawed
1 to 2 (4 oz. cans) MUSHROOMS, drained
1 can CREAM OF MUSHROOM SOUP
1 can CREAM OF CHICKEN SOUP
1/2 cup MAYONNAISE
1/2 cup MILK
1/2 cup SOUR CREAM
1 cup CHEDDAR CHEESE, grated
1 cup MONTEREY JACK, grated
2 Tbsp. LEMON JUICE
BUTTERED FINE DRY BREAD CRUMBS, plain or Italian

Cook chicken breasts in water 30 minutes; drain. When cool enough to handle, discard skin and bones. Pull chicken into large chunks and arrange in 9 x 13 baking pan. Sprinkle evenly with broccoli. In large bowl, combine mushrooms, soup, mayonnaise, milk, sour cream, cheeses and lemon juice. Mix well and spread evenly over chicken and broccoli. Cover with buttered crumbs; bake at 350 degrees for one hour. Serves 6 to 8. May be made ahead and refrigerated, but allow longer baking time.

If chicken sounds good, head for Springfield's barbecue in mid-July. The Oregon Broilers Festival is one of the Northwest's largest feasts. Without ever leaving town, you can also fish for trout and steelhead, and take a whitewater ride.

McMinnville 'Turkeyrama' Tetrazzini

1 cube BUTTER
1 lg. GREEN PEPPER, chopped
2 cans MUSHROOM PIECES
1 sm. jar PIMIENTOS
1 tsp. each SALT and PEPPER
1 1/2 tsp. WORCESTERSHIRE SAUCE
3 Tbsp. FLOUR
1/2 cup DRY SHERRY
2 cups MILK
2 cans CREAM OF MUSHROOM SOUP
1/2 tsp. GARLIC POWDER
6 cups COOKED TURKEY (or CHICKEN)
3 cups CHEDDAR CHEESE, grated, divided
1 1/2 cups GRATED PARMESAN CHEESE, divided
1 lb. SPAGHETTI, cooked

Melt butter in large pot; add green pepper. Cook for a few minutes until softened. Add mushrooms and pimientos; continue to sauté. Add salt, pepper, Worcestershire sauce and flour; stir together and add sherry, milk and soup. Stir and heat; add garlic powder, turkey, 2 1/2 cups cheddar cheese and one cup parmesan cheese; mix. Add cooked hot spaghetti, mix together. Pour into casserole dish, top with remaining cheeses. Place in 350 degree oven to heat thoroughly, 30 to 45 minutes.

McMinnville was crowned in 1962 as the "Turkey Capital of the World." For three days each July, the city celebrates Turkeyrama. One of the events, the Biggest Turkey Talent Show, draws hundreds of spectators for this zany happening. The annual turkey barbecue draws huge crowds.

Standing Rib Roast with Yorkshire Pudding

4 to 6 lbs. (2 to 3 ribs) BEEF RIB ROAST, small end
SALT and PEPPER
2 EGGS

1 cup MILK
1/2 tsp. SALT
1 cup FLOUR
HORSERADISH SAUCE

Place roast bone-side down in open roasting pan. Sprinkle with salt and pepper. Place meat thermometer in the thickest part of the roast making sure it is not in contact with a bone. Bake in 325 degree oven until internal temperature reaches 160 degrees, for medium doneness, (2 1/4 to 3 1/2 hours). When roast is done, allow to stand at room temperature for 15 minutes before carving. In a medium bowl with a wire whisk, beat eggs until foamy. Beat in milk and salt; gradually beat in flour until batter is smooth. When roast is done, spoon off 2 tablespoons of drippings, and divide into 12 three-inch muffin cups. Tilt to coat evenly. Heat muffin pan in oven for 5 minutes at 400 degrees. Remove and pour 2 1/2 Tbsp. batter into each greased muffin cup. Bake 30 minutes at 400 degrees; loosen and serve with roast and horseradish sauce.

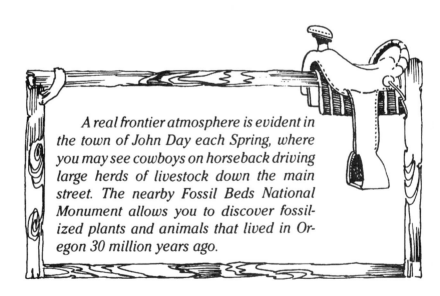

A real frontier atmosphere is evident in the town of John Day each Spring, where you may see cowboys on horseback driving large herds of livestock down the main street. The nearby Fossil Beds National Monument allows you to discover fossilized plants and animals that lived in Oregon 30 million years ago.

Gobblin' Good Taco Bake

1 lb. GROUND TURKEY
1 (14 oz. can) MILD ENCHILADA SAUCE
1 can CREAM OF MUSHROOM SOUP
1/4 tsp. GARLIC POWDER
1/2 cup ONION, chopped
1 (8 oz. pkg.) CORN CHIPS
4 oz. AMERICAN or CHEDDAR CHEESE, grated
1 can SLICED RIPE OLIVES

Brown turkey; drain if necessary. Stir in enchilada sauce, soup, garlic powder and onion; grease a 7 x 12 casserole dish. Sprinkle with 2/3 of the corn chips, pour turkey mixture over chips. Sprinkle with cheese, then remaining corn chips and olives. Bake at 350 degrees, 35 to 40 minutes until heated through. Serves 4.

Following a bear into an entrance, Elijah Davidson discovered the Oregon Caves in 1874. The caves were declared a national monument by President Taft in 1909. It is a rare marble cave, filled with incredible changing formations.

Favorite Pork Chop Dinner

5 PORK CHOPS
SALT and PEPPER to taste
1 (23 oz. can) SWEET POTATOES, drained
3/4 cup MAPLE FLAVOR SYRUP
1 can REFRIGERATED BISCUITS

Brown pork chops; place in 9 x 13 ungreased pan. Season with salt and pepper; cover and bake 20 minutes at 375 degrees. Remove from oven; drain. Move pork chops to one side of pan, arrange potatoes around pork chops. Pour syrup over chops and potatoes; arrange biscuits in pan next to chops and potatoes. Bake uncovered an additional 20 to 25 minutes until biscuits are golden brown and chops are tender.

Baker City Biscuit Bake

1 lb. GROUND BEEF
1/4 cup ONION, chopped
4 oz. CHEESE, grated
2 Tbsp. PARSLEY, snipped
1 1/2 cups PREPARED BISCUIT MIX
1/2 cup MILK

Vegetable Sauce:
  1 can MUSHROOM SOUP
  1/3 cup MILK
  1 can MIXED VEGETABLES, drained

Brown beef and onion; drain. Stir in cheese and parsley; set aside. Combine biscuit mix and milk, knead 8 to 10 times. Divide dough into two 8-inch circles. Press one circle into well-greased cake pan, spread meat on top. Place second biscuit on top. Bake at 375 degrees for 20 to 25 minutes. Cut into wedges, serve with vegetable sauce.

In 1861, stories of an Oregon stream heavy with gold pebbles brought excited prospectors to the creeks and gulleys near Baker City. Today, the city has over 135 buildings listed on the National Register of Historic Places.

Turkey Wonder

1 can CHINESE NOODLES
2 cups TURKEY
1 cup WATER
1 cup CELERY, chopped
    in large pieces
1 can MUSHROOM SOUP

1 can MUSHROOMS
CASHEWS, chopped
1/2 cup ONIONS, chopped
CRUSHED POTATO CHIPS
GRATED CHEESE

Place noodles in bottom of casserole; mix remaining ingredients (except potato chips and cheese) and cover noodles. Top with finely crushed potato chips and grated cheese. Heat oven to 350 degrees, bake until heated through (about 30 minutes). Serves 6.

Creamy Turkey Pie

1 lb. GROUND TURKEY
1/2 cup ONION, diced
1 (3 oz. pkg.) CREAM CHEESE, cubed
1 (4 1/2 oz. jar) MUSHROOMS, sliced, drained
1 pkg. REFRIGERATED BISCUITS
1 EGG
1 cup COTTAGE CHEESE
1 Tbsp. FLOUR
DICED TOMATO, for garnish

In large skillet, cook turkey and onion until meat is browned. Drain fat; stir in cream cheese till combined. Add mushrooms and set aside. For the crust, lightly grease 9-inch pie plate; separate biscuits and arrange on bottom and up the sides of the plate extending about 1/2 inch above pie plate. Spoon turkey into shell, spreading evenly. In blender, combine egg, cottage cheese and flour. Cover and blend until smooth; spoon over turkey mix. Bake uncovered 350 degrees for 25 to 30 minutes until edges brown and filling is set. Let stand 5 minutes. Garnish with tomato.

> *Can you imagine racing a Model T Ford while holding a pig on your lap? It's only one of the events that happens every summer just south of Rockaway as the Tillamook County Fair comes alive.*

Old Fashioned Baked Ham

Margie Tiegs — Rockaway Beach Chamber of Commerce

1 HAM
WATER to cover
1/4 cup SUGAR
2 Tbsp. VINEGAR
WHOLE CLOVES
2 cups BREAD CRUMBS
2 Tbsp. BROWN SUGAR
2 Tbsp. MOLASSES
2 tsp. PREPARED MUSTARD
2 Tbsp. BUTTER

Wash ham and cover with water. To each quart of water used, add 1/4 cup sugar and 2 Tbsp. vinegar. Simmer until tender; let ham remain in broth until cool. Skin ham and stick cloves in one inch intervals. Combine remaining ingredients and spread on ham. Bake in 325 degree oven until brown. Baste ham with broth during baking.

Chicken Strata

BUTTER
16 slices DRY BREAD, dried in oven
4 cups COOKED CHICKEN, diced
1 lg. ONION, chopped
1 lg. GREEN PEPPER, chopped
1 cup CELERY, chopped
1 cup MAYONNAISE
1/2 Tbsp. SALT
3 EGGS, beaten
3 cups MILK
2 cans CREAM OF MUSHROOM SOUP
1 cup CHEESE, grated

Butter 1/4 of bread slices; cut into 1/2 inch cubes and set aside. Cut remaining bread in one inch cubes; place half of unbuttered bread in 9 x 13 pan. Combine next 6 ingredients and spoon over bread cubes. Sprinkle remaining unbuttered cubes over chicken mixture. Combine eggs and milk and pour over all. Cover, chill one hour or overnight. Spoon soup over top, sprinkle with buttered cubes. Bake at 325 degrees for 50 to 60 minutes. Sprinkle grated cheese over top during the last few minutes. Serves 12.

Microwave Chili

Bob McCarthy — Rockaway Beach

1 lb. lean GROUND BEEF
1 med. ONION, chopped
1 clove GARLIC, minced
1 (7 1/2 oz. can) TOMATO SAUCE
1 (14 oz. can) WHOLE ITALIAN
    TOMATOES, cut up, undrained

1 Tbsp. CHILI POWDER
1 tsp. CUMIN
1 tsp. SUGAR
1 tsp. SALT
1/4 tsp. PEPPER
1 can KIDNEY BEANS

Crumble ground beef in 3 qt. casserole; add onion and garlic. Microwave 4 to 5 minutes on high until beef is no longer pink. Stir to break meat apart after half cooking time. Combine remaining ingredients, mix well and add to beef. Microwave on high 5 minutes; stir and cover. Microwave 20 to 25 minutes, stirring once or twice. Serve with grated cheese, green onion, sour cream, etc.

Stuffed Macaroni Shells

1/2 cup ONION, chopped
1/2 tsp. GARLIC, minced
1/2 lb. GROUND BEEF
1 (15 oz. can) TOMATO SAUCE
1 (6 oz. can) TOMATO PASTE
1/2 tsp. SALT
1/2 tsp. OREGANO
1/4 tsp. PEPPER

1 1/2 cups COTTAGE CHEESE
1 EGG
1/4 cup PARMESAN CHEESE
2 Tbsp. FRESH PARSLEY
sprinkle NUTMEG
JUMBO MACARONI SHELLS
   (about 18), cooked, drained

Cook first 3 ingredients about 5 minutes. Pour off any fat. Stir in next 5 ingredients. Bring to a simmer; turn heat down and cook about 15 minutes. Meanwhile in medium size bowl, combine next 5 ingredients; heat oven to 350 degrees. Spread 2 1/2 cups of tomato sauce mixture in oblong 2 qt. baking dish. Using a spoon, fill each cooked shell with the cheese mixture. Arrange stuffed shells on tomato sauce, and top each with a spoonful of remaining sauce. Bake 25 to 30 minutes until hot. Serves 4 to 6.

> *"A million head of cattle and a million acres of land" was typical of the early day cattle barons in Oregon. Burns was the unofficial capital of the 19th century cattle empires on the high desert plateaus of eastern Oregon.*

Chili Meatballs

1 1/2 lbs. GROUND BEEF
1 ONION, chopped
1 tsp. SALT
1/4 tsp. PEPPER

1/2 GREEN PEPPER, chopped
1 to 2 tsp. CHILI POWDER
1 (15 oz. can) TOMATO SAUCE

Combine ground beef with 1/2 cup of chopped onion, salt and pepper. Form into 16 meatballs. Brown meatballs with green pepper and remaining onion. Combine chili powder with tomato sauce; pour over meatballs in skillet. Simmer 15 to 20 minutes. Serve with spaghetti. Serves 4.

Chicken Cacciatore

1/4 cup FLOUR
1 tsp. SALT
1/4 tsp. PEPPER
3 to 3 1/2 lbs. FRYING CHICKEN PIECES
1/4 cup SALAD OIL
1/2 cup ONION, chopped
1 3/4 cups (14.5 oz. can) WHOLE PEELED TOMATOES, and juice
2/3 cup (6 oz. can) TOMATO PASTE
1 (4 oz. can) SLICED MUSHROOMS, and liquid
1 clove GARLIC, crushed
1/2 cup WATER
1/2 tsp. ITALIAN SEASONING
1/4 tsp. OREGANO LEAVES

Combine flour, salt and pepper. Coat chicken with flour mixture; in large skillet brown chicken in oil. Pour off excess fat; combine remaining ingredients, stirring to break up tomatoes. Pour over chicken, cover and boil gently for 45 minutes or until chicken is tender. Remove chicken to serving dish; thicken remaining sauce if desired. Serve with cooked pasta. Serves 6.

Fort Stevens, near Warrenton, is the only military installation in the continental U. S. to be fired on since 1812. On June 12, 1942, a Japanese submarine fired 17 shells toward the fort, but caused no damage, and fire was not returned.

Gingered Spare Ribs

1/2 cup BROWN SUGAR
1 env. DRY ITALIAN
      DRESSING MIX
1 tsp. CELERY SALT
1 1/2 tsp. GINGER

1/2 cup CATSUP
1/4 cup VINEGAR
1/2 cup WATER
2 to 3 lbs. COUNTRY STYLE
      SPARE RIBS

Combine dry ingredients; in small bowl, mix catsup, vinegar and water. Then add to the dry mixture and mix well. Place ribs on barbecue, or bake in oven, basting every 15 minutes.

Klamath Roast Beef

Sylvia Gillette — Klamath Falls

4 lbs. BONELESS CHUCK or RUMP ROAST
2 Tbsp. FLOUR
2 tsp. SEASONING SALT
1 tsp. PEPPER
2 Tbsp. OIL
2 cups ONION, sliced
1/2 cup WATER
1/4 cup RED WINE VINEGAR
1/4 cup CATSUP
2 tsp. BEEF SOUP MIX
1 1/2 tsp. THYME
1 tsp. DRY MUSTARD
8 CARROTS, halved
4 POTATOES, halved
1 (6 oz. can) SLICED MUSHROOMS, drained
1/4 cup WATER
2 Tbsp. FLOUR

Dredge meat in flour, seasoning salt and pepper. In a Dutch oven, brown meats on both sides in oil. Add onion; combine cold water, vinegar, catsup, soup mix, thyme and dry mustard. Add to meat; simmer covered for 1 1/2 hours, add carrots and potatoes and more water if needed. Simmer covered another 30 to 45 minutes. Remove meat and vegetables to platter; skim excess fat from pan juices. Add mushrooms. Blend together remaining cold water and flour and stir into juices. Cook and stir over medium heat until thickened and bubbly. Serves 8 to 10.

One of Oregon's leading cattle raising areas is Fort Klamath. The fort was built in 1863 to protect wagon trains from Indian attacks.

Oven Biscuit Stew

1/4 cup MARGARINE
1/3 cup FLOUR
1/2 tsp. SALT
dash PEPPER
1 (10 3/4 oz. can) CHICKEN BROTH
3/4 cup MILK
2 cups CHICKEN, cooked, chopped
1/3 cup ONION, chopped
1 can PEAS, drained
1 can WHOLE BABY CARROTS, drained
1 can REFRIGERATED BISCUITS

Heat oven to 375 degrees. In 10-inch skillet, melt margarine; blend in flour, salt and pepper. Add broth and milk, cook, stirring until thick. In mixing bowl, combine chicken, onion, peas and carrots. Add to the hot mixture. Simmer until hot and bubbly. Place mixture in baking dish with biscuits on top and bake for 20 to 25 minutes.

Baked Manicotti

1 (5 1/2 oz. pkg.) MANICOTTI
1 lb. RICOTTA CHEESE
1/2 lb. MOZZARELLA CHEESE, grated
3/4 cup PARMESAN CHEESE, divided into 1/2 cup and 1/4 cup
2 EGGS, beaten
1 tsp. PARSLEY, chopped
SALT and PEPPER to taste
1 (15 1/2 oz. jar) SPAGHETTI SAUCE WITH MUSHROOMS

Preheat oven to 350 degrees; cook manicotti as package directs and drain. Set aside. Combine cheeses except 1/4 cup parmesan, eggs, parsley, salt and pepper; mix well. Into an 11 x 7 baking dish, pour 1/2 cup spaghetti sauce. Fill manicotti with about 3 Tbsp. cheese mixture and arrange over sauce. Pour remaining sauce on top, and sprinkle with 1/4 cup parmesan cheese. Bake 45 minutes until bubbly. Serves 4.

Skillet Chicken Supreme

1 tsp. SEASONING SALT
1/4 tsp. PEPPER
2 1/2 to 3 lbs. CHICKEN PIECES
1/4 cup OIL
1 ONION, chopped
1/4 lb. FRESH MUSHROOMS, sliced
1 Tbsp. FLOUR
1 can CREAM OF MUSHROOM SOUP
1 cup EVAPORATED MILK
2 (10 oz. pkgs.) FROZEN GREEN BEANS, thawed

Sprinkle salt and pepper over chicken; heat oil in large skillet and brown chicken on all sides. Remove chicken from skillet; set aside. Drain all but one tablespoon fat, add onions and mushrooms to skillet. Sauté until onion is tender; stir in flour and add soup and milk, mixing thoroughly. Place chicken in skillet, cover and boil gently 45 minutes to one hour until tender. Stir to prevent sticking. Add green beans and heat an additional 15 minutes.

Macaroni & Beef Casserole

1 lb. GROUND BEEF
1 sm. GREEN PEPPER, diced
1 med. ONION, diced
1 1/2 tsp. SALT
1/4 tsp. PEPPER
1 (8 oz. pkg.) ELBOW
   MACARONI, uncooked
1 (16 oz. can) TOMATOES
1 can TOMATO SOUP
1/2 tsp. SUGAR

Preheat oven to 350 degrees. In 10-inch skillet over high heat, cook first 5 ingredients until meat is browned, about 10 minutes. Remove from heat; spoon mixture into 2 qt. casserole. Add uncooked macaroni, tomatoes (with liquid) and remaining ingredients to casserole. Stir to break up tomatoes. Cover; bake 35 minutes or until mixture is hot and macaroni is tender. Stir occasionally. Serves 6.

Teriyaki Pork Chops

4 PORK CHOPS, 1/2 to 3/4 inch thick
1/2 cup BOTTLED TERIYAKI SAUCE
1 Tbsp. FLOUR
1 cup UNCOOKED RICE
1/2 cup ONION, chopped
1 med. GREEN PEPPER, cut into 1" squares
1 (4 oz. can) MUSHROOM STEMS & PIECES
1 (6 ox. can) PINEAPPLE JUICE
1/3 cup WATER

Place pork chops in regular size oven cooking bag. Place bag in 9 x 13 baking pan. Pour teriyaki sauce over the chops; turn bag gently to coat with sauce. Arrange chops in a single layer, marinating at room temperature for one hour. After marinating, remove from bag and set aside. Add remaining ingredients to bag and squeeze gently to blend with the flour. Return pork chops in single layer to bag. Close with a nylon tie. Make 6 half-inch slits in bag top; bake at 325 degrees for 45 to 55 minutes or until tender.

Mexi-Beef Loaf

2 lbs. GROUND BEEF
1 Tbsp. CHILI POWDER
1 tsp. SALT
1/2 tsp. CUMIN
1 med. ONION, chopped
1/2 cup SOFT BREAD CRUMBS
1/4 cup PIMIENTO STUFFED OLIVES, chopped
1 EGG, slightly beaten
1 (8 oz. can) TOMATO SAUCE
2 Tbsp. CHEDDAR CHEESE, grated
2 to 4 STUFFED OLIVES, sliced

Over ground beef, sprinkle chili powder, salt and cumin. Add onion, bread crumbs, olives, egg and tomato sauce, mixing lightly but thoroughly. Press meat mixture into 9 x 5 loaf pan; turn loaf out onto rack in open roasting pan. Bake at 350 degrees for one hour or until done. Sprinkle cheese over top of loaf, garnish with sliced olives if desired. Let stand 10 minutes before serving. Serves 6.

Round-Up Beef Pie

1 lb. GROUND CHUCK
1 (8 oz. can) MUSHROOMS, drained
1 Tbsp. SALAD OIL
2 pkgs. FROZEN SPINACH or BROCCOLI,
       chopped, cooked, drained
1 can CREAM OF CELERY SOUP
1 cup SOUR CREAM
1 tsp. GARLIC SALT
1/2 tsp. PEPPER
5 tsp. ONION, minced
1 (6 oz.) MOZZARELLA CHEESE, sliced

Preheat oven at 350 degrees. Brown beef and mushrooms in oil. Spoon into a 2 qt. casserole; stir in spinach, soup, sour cream and seasonings. Cut sliced cheese into strips and place on top of casserole. Do not cover. Bake at 350 degrees for 35 to 45 minutes. Serves 4.

"The Round-Up City", Pendleton, says it is not the New West, not the Old West, but the REAL West. Every September, the Pendleton Round-Up rodeo plays to packed houses. The Pendleton Woolen Mills allow tourists to see wool being made into sweaters through the carding, spinning, weaving and dyeing processes.

Easy Stew

1 lb. STEW MEAT
3 med. POTATOES, peeled
    and cubed

3 CARROTS, peeled and diced
1 can MUSHROOM SOUP
1 can CELERY SOUP

Place stew meat, potatoes and carrots in greased casserole dish. Combine soups and pour over top. Cover and bake at 325 degrees for 3 1/2 hours.

Chili Relleno Bake

1 lb. GROUND BEEF
1/2 cup ONION, chopped
SALT and PEPPER to taste
2 (4 oz. cans) WHOLE GREEN CHILES, drained
6 oz. SHARP CHEESE, grated
1 1/2 cups MILK
4 EGGS, well beaten
1/4 cup FLOUR
1/2 tsp. SALT
several dashes HOT PEPPER SAUCE

Brown beef with onion, salt and pepper; drain off grease. Halve the chiles and remove the seeds. Place half of the chiles in a 10 x 6 x 1 1/2 baking dish; sprinkle with grated cheese. Place meat mixture on top. Lay balance of chiles on top of meat. Combine milk, eggs, flour, salt and pepper sauce and beat until smooth. Pour over the chiles. Bake at 350 degrees for 45 to 50 minutes, until knife inserted in center comes out clean. Cool 5 minutes before serving. Serves 6.

Acres and acres of vegetables are harvested annually in the Hermiston area. Nearby, the Columbia River meanders lazily north into Washington's Yakima Valley.

Tamale Pie

1 1/2 cups CORN CHIPS, crushed
3 (15 oz. cans) TAMALES
3 (15 oz. cans) CHILI WITHOUT BEANS
1 (8 1/2 oz. can) WHOLE KERNEL CORN, undrained
1/3 cup GREEN PEPPER, chopped, sautéed until tender
CHEDDAR CHEESE, grated, (amount to taste)

Cover bottom of 9 x 13 baking pan with chips. Remove paper from tamales and arrange over chips in 2 rows. Heat chili until hot; add corn and green pepper and pour over the tamales. Cover and bake at 325 degrees for 25 minutes. Uncover; sprinkle with grated cheese and return to oven for 10 minutes. Serves 8.

Cornish Game Hen with Wild Blackberry Sauce

Chetco River Inn — Brookings

4 WHOLE CORNISH GAME HENS
1/4 tsp. CUMIN
1/4 tsp. OREGANO
1/4 tsp. THYME
1/2 tsp. GARLIC POWDER
1/2 tsp. BLACK PEPPER
1 tsp. SALT
1/8 tsp. CINNAMON
1 cup BLACKBERRIES
1/4 cup SHERRY
1/4 cup SOY SAUCE
1 tsp. GARLIC POWDER
1 cup WATER

Season hens by rubbing mixture of spices on skin. Roast on rack in pan at 350 degrees for 30 minutes. Combine berries, sherry, soy sauce and garlic powder and baste hens. Add water to the pan; cover hens with oiled foil or pan cover. Bake 45 minutes to one hour; drain liquid. Reduce hen juices; baste again before serving. Serve with pan juices over rice.

*A half hour drive from Brookings (first town in Oregon when traveling north on scenic Highway 101) brings you to another world at **Chetco River Inn.** Bird watching, fishing, swimming and hiking beckon the traveler to return. Meals here are a special treat, since owner Sandra Brugger researches new recipes, and enlivens them with her own talents.*

Krautkucken

(German Kraut Buns)

Dorothy Markell — Portland

Cool rise white bread:
- **7 3/4 to 8 cups FLOUR**
- **3 Tbsp. SUGAR**
- **4 tsp. SALT**
- **3 pkgs. DRY YEAST**
- **1/3 cup SOFT MARGARINE**
- **2 2/3 cup WATER, very warm**

Filling:
- **1 lb. GROUND BEEF**
- **1 1/2 heads CABBAGE, chopped**
- **2 med. ONIONS, chopped**

Mix 3 cups flour in large bowl, and rest of ingredients. Beat by mixer or by hand for a few minutes; then, add 1/2 cup flour and beat again. Stir in flour gradually to make a stiff dough. Turn out on lightly floured board and knead 10 to 12 minutes. Cover with plastic wrap and then a towel; let rest 20 minutes and store in refrigerator. When ready to bake remove from referigerator and uncover carefully. Let stand 10 minutes. Punch any bubbles. To make filling, brown and drain meat. Cook vegetables in small amount of oil, not browned. Cool the mixture. Roll dough to about 1/8 inch thick and cut into rectangles about 4 1/2 inches to 5 1/2 inches, spread with margarine. Combine cooled, cooked vegetables with meat and season to taste. Spoon onto dough and pull edges over filling, pinching to seal. Place seam side down on greased sheet and bake at 375 degrees until golden brown.

Portland ranks among the nation's top wheat ports. The northern and central regions of the state are especially known for wheat production, producing some of the finest flours available.

Spaghetti Pie

8 oz. SPAGHETTI, cooked, drained
2 Tbsp. BUTTER
2 lg. EGGS, well beaten
1/2 cup plus 2 Tbsp. PARMESAN CHEESE, grated
1 cup RICOTTA CHEESE
1 cup SPAGHETTI SAUCE
1/2 cup MOZZARELLA CHEESE, grated

Heat oven to 350 degrees. In large bowl, toss hot spaghetti with butter. In small bowl, combine eggs and 1/2 cup parmesan. Stir into spaghetti. Pour spaghetti mixture into a lightly greased 10-inch pie plate, and form into a crust. Spread ricotta evenly over the crust, but not quite to the edge and top with spaghetti sauce. Bake uncovered for 25 minutes. Remove from oven; top with mozzarella. Return to oven and bake 5 more minutes until cheese melts. Remove from oven and sprinkle with remaining parmesan. Cool 10 minutes before cutting into wedges.

The main street of Sisters is lined with western store fronts providing an appealing stop for travelers in horseless carriages. It also has hitching posts where you can tie up your horse, if you're on horseback.

Oregon Seafoods

Columbia River Salmon in Hazelnut Butter

3 Tbsp. unsalted BUTTER
6 (7 oz.) SALMON FILLETS
SALT and PEPPER to taste
1 1/2 cups FISH STOCK
1 1/2 Tbsp. LEMON JUICE
1/2 cup HAZELNUT BUTTER

Select a baking sheet large enough to hold fillets, and deep enough to hold the liquid. Coat sheet with butter; lightly salt and pepper fillets. Lay them in pan, add fish stock and lemon juice. Place a dollop of hazelnut butter on top of each fillet. Bake in 500 degree oven for 10 minutes. Remove salmon from oven, place fillets on individual heated plates. Pour liquid from baking sheet into a sauté pan and bring to a boil. Add remaining hazelnut butter to the pan; simmer until sauce has thickened. Divide sauce equally among fillets, and serve immediately. Hazelnut butter is available at specialty food stores. Serves 6.

Shrimp Quiche

1/2 cup MAYONNAISE
2 Tbsp. FLOUR
2 EGGS, beaten
1/2 cup MILK
1 cup fresh or canned SHRIMP

1/3 cup GREEN ONION, chopped
1 Tbsp, PARSLEY, minced
2 cups shredded SWISS CHEESE
1 9-inch PIE SHELL, unbaked

In mixing bowl, combine mayonnaise, flour, eggs and milk, mixing well. Stir in shrimp, onion, parsley and cheese. Spoon into pie shell and bake for one hour at 350 degrees.

Dill Salmon Encroute

Lee Century Farms — Milton-Freewater

PUFF PASTRY SHEETS
1 EGG
3 to 8 slices DILL HAVARTI CHEESE
6 (4 oz.) FRESH SALMON FILLETS
1/2 to 3/4 cup DILL WHEATBERRY CAVIAR
LEMON PEPPER

Cut puff pastry sheets into 6 x 6 inch squares. Lightly beat the egg with 2 tablespoons of water and brush over the squares. Place one square of cheese on each, next the salmon, and top with 2 tablespoons of Dill Wheatberry Caviar. Sprinkle with lemon pepper. Fold pastry over and be sure to seal well. Turn over and brush the top with egg mixture. Repeat with each salmon fillet. Bake at 375 degrees for 10 to 15 minutes.

High in north-eastern Oregon, Milton-Freewater vegetable stands offer fresh apricots, asparagus, peas, corn, cherries, peaches, pears and those famous Walla Walla onions. The city maintains its own electrical power, providing residents with one of the lowest rates in the Northwest.

Tillamook Seafood & Cheese Linguine

6 to 8 oz. LINGUINE, or other pasta
2 lg. cloves GARLIC, minced
1 tsp. DRIED OREGANO, crushed
2 Tbsp. MARGARINE
1 med. TOMATO, chopped
1/2 cup WHIPPING CREAM
1 (6 or 8 oz. pkg.) IMITATION CRAB MEAT or
    LOBSTER FLAKES or CHUNKS
1/2 cup GREEN ONION, sliced, with tops
1/4 cup BLEU CHEESE, crumbled or SWISS CHEESE, grated
1/4 cup PARMESAN or ROMANO CHEESE

Cook pasta according to directions; drain. While pasta cooks, in a saucepan sauté garlic and oregano in margarine for one minute, stirring frequently. Add tomato, continue cooking, stirring occasionally for 3 minutes until tomato is cooked through. Add remaining ingredients and mix well. Cook over medium heat, stirring frequently, until cheese is melted and sauce is hot. Place hot cooked pasta on serving plate, top with sauce. Serves 3 or 4.

Cheese making is big business in Tillamook, home of the West's largest cheese plant. More than 200,000 visitors a year sample the famous cheeses. The world's largest clear span wood building houses the most World War II fighter planes in the Northwest. It takes a tractor to open the doors of this building, which is large enough to accommodate six football games at one time.

Haddock Shrimp Bake

Lois Stevens — Rockaway Beach

2 lbs. FROZEN HADDOCK (thick fish, slightly thawed)
1 (10 1/2 oz. can) CREAM OF POTATO SOUP
3/4 cup MILK
1 cup FROZEN COOKED SHRIMP
1/4 cup BUTTER. melted
1/2 tsp. ONION, grated
1/2 tsp. WORCESTERSHIRE SAUCE
1/4 tsp. GARLIC SALT
1 1/4 cups RITZ® CRACKER CRUMBS (about 30)

Place fish in greased 9 x 13 x 2 baking dish. Heat soup with milk and stir in shrimp. Spread over fish; bake at 375 degrees for 20 minutes. Combine all remaining ingredients, except cracker crumbs, and pour over fish. Sprinkle crumbs over all and bake 10 minutes. Serves 6 to 8.

Barbecue Fish Fillets

5 Tbsp. MARGARINE, divided
1/2 cup DICED ONION
1 lb. FISH FILLETS
SALT and PEPPER
1/2 cup CATSUP
1/3 cup LEMON JUICE
2 tsp. SUGAR
2 tsp. WORCESTERSHIRE SAUCE
2 tsp. PREPARED MUSTARD
1/4 cup WATER

Heat electric fry pan to 300 degrees; melt 2 tablespoons margarine and add onions, frying till brown. Remove from skillet. Add remainder of margarine; turn skillet to 360 degrees and brown fillets, turning once. Spread onions over fish, and salt and pepper to taste. Combine remaining ingredients with water; pour over fish and simmer at 220 degrees for 20 minutes.

Crispy Fish Fillets

1 cup MILK
1/2 tsp. SALT
1 cup CORN MEAL or variety baking mix
1/4 cup VEGETABLE OIL
1 lb. FISH FILLETS

Mix milk and salt in small bowl; place corn meal in pie pan. Heat oil in 10-inch skillet over medium heat. Using tongs, dip fish in milk mixture, then in corn meal. Fry fish in hot oil over medium heat about 5 minutes on each side or until fish flakes easily with fork. Do not overcook. Drain on paper towels. For a change of taste, try serving with *Creole Sauce* below.

Creole Sauce

3 Tbsp. OIL
2 Tbsp. ONION, chopped
2 Tbsp. GREEN PEPPER, chopped
1/4 cup SLICED MUSHROOMS
2 cups STEWED TOMATOES

1/2 tsp. SALT
dash PEPPER
few drops TABASCO®
   SAUCE
1/2 tsp. BASIL

Cook onion, green pepper and mushrooms in oil over low heat for about 5 minutes. Add tomatoes and seasonings and simmer until sauce is thick, about 30 minutes.

Scalloped Salmon

1 (16 oz. can) SALMON,
   undrained
2 EGGS
1 cup MILK

1 sm. ONION, diced fine
1 cup SODA CRACKERS, crushed
1/2 cup CELERY, diced
1/2 cup GREEN PEPPER, diced

Mix all ingredients together, breaking salmon into small pieces and place in buttered casserole dish. Bake one hour at 350 degrees.

Razor Clam Pie

Clam Mixture:
- **1 lg. ONION, chopped**
- **2 Tbsp. BUTTER**
- **1/2 pt. CHOPPED RAZOR CLAMS**
- **1 to 2 ribs CELERY, chopped**
- **1 lg. POTATO, diced**
- **1 Tbsp. PARSLEY FLAKES**
- **1/3 lb. BACON, cooked, drained, crumbled**

Sauce:
- **2 Tbsp. BUTTER**
- **3 Tbsp. FLOUR**
- **1/2 cup VERMOUTH**
- **1/2 cup EVAPORATED MILK**
- **1/2 tsp. SALT**
- **1/4 tsp. PEPPER**
- **1/8 tsp. NUTMEG**
- **dash PEPPER SAUCE**

Pastry:
- **1 1/2 cups FLOUR**
- **1/4 tsp. SALT**
- **6 Tbsp. BUTTER**
- **2 Tbsp. SHORTENING**
- **4 Tbsp. COLD WATER**

Sauté onion in butter for 10 minutes; add clams, vegetables, parsley and bacon and cook 5 more minutes. In saucepan, melt butter and stir in flour and vermouth. Stir until smooth; pour in milk and again stir until smooth. Add salt, pepper, nutmeg and pepper sauce; combine sauce with clam mixture. Make a 10-inch pie shell, top and bottom, with pastry ingredients. Pour combined sauce and clam mixture into bottom shell; add top. Bake for 10 minutes at 400 degrees. Reduce heat to 350 and bake an additional 40 minutes. Let stand 30 minutes before cutting. Serves 6.

Barbecue Cooked Salmon

WHOLE SALMON
SALT
1 box BROWN SUGAR
1 to 2 LEMONS
1 cube BUTTER or MARGARINE

Cut whole salmon lengthwise into halves, removing backbone. Leave skin and scales on. Salt meat heavily, pat brown sugar on thickly. Dot with thick pats of butter. Sprinkle with lemon juice. When coals are really hot, place fish on grill, skin side down. When butter starts to melt, cover fish with foil. Cook 10 to 15 minutes more, depending on size of fish. Do not overcook. Remove meat to platter. Skin will remain on grill and salmon should still be very pink and moist.

Clam digging, kite flying, surf fishing, and eating ice cream cones are favorite pastimes when visitors descend on Haystack Rock. Rising 235 feet above the ocean, the world's most photographed offshore monolith lures photographers to Cannon Beach. It also serves as a wildlife refuge and its tide pools are home to starfish, anemones, crabs, limpets, and chitons. Sculptors of all ages turn the spacious beach into a sand castle construction site each year.

Salmon Steaks

6 (3/4 inch) SALMON STEAKS
1/3 cup BUTTER, melted
1/2 tsp. SALT
1/4 tsp. PAPRIKA
1 tsp. WORCESTERSHIRE SAUCE

1 tsp. PREPARED MUSTARD
2 Tbsp. SOY SAUCE
2 Tbsp. CATSUP
1 clove GARLIC, minced

Arrange steaks in single layer in greased 10 x 15 inch baking pan. Combine next four ingredients; spoon over steaks. Bake uncovered at 350 degrees for 20 minutes, or until fish flakes easily in thickest part when pierced with fork. Remove fish to warm serving platter and keep warm. Place drippings into a saucepan; stir in mustard, soy sauce, catsup and garlic. Cook over medium heat until bubbly; spoon over salmon. Serves 6.

Portland, "The City of Roses", is also a city of parks, fountains, gardens and jazz. Dividing the city in halves, the Willamette River flows into the Columbia River north of town. More than 10,000 rose bushes in the International Rose Test Gardens bloom each summer. There is also a peaceful Shakespearean Garden, said to contain examples of every plant mentioned in the Bard's plays. The Portland Rose Festival is culminated each year with the famed Grande Floral Parade in June.

Barbecue Marinade for Salmon

4 oz. BUTTER
juice of 2 LEMONS
2 Tbsp. WORCESTERSHIRE SAUCE
2 tsp. SALT

2 tsp. PEPPER
1 tsp. DRY MUSTARD
2 tsp. GARLIC SALT

Melt butter, add other ingredients and blend. Brush sauce on fillet about one hour before barbecuing. Barbecue fish over alder coals (or briquets) in a fish holder and baste with sauce. Do not overcook.

Oysters Rigatoni

4 oz. DRY RIGATONI
1/2 YELLOW ONION, thinly sliced
4 med. FRESH CHANTERELLES, sliced
2 Tbsp. OLIVE OIL
2 Tbsp. BUTTER
1 doz. sm. OYSTERS, freshly shucked
1 Tbsp. FRESH OREGANO
3 to 4 Tbsp. DRY SHERRY
1/4 cup HALF AND HALF
1 Tbsp. ITALIAN PARSLEY, fresh, minced
3 slices TUSCAN SALAMI, julienned
SALT and PEPPER to taste

Cook pasta in boiling salted water. While cooking, sauté onions and chanterelles in oil and butter. When soft, add oysters, their juice, and oregano. Cook over medium heat for 1 minute. Turn heat to high and add sherry. As soon as alcohol has evaporated, turn heat down and add half and half. Heat through; add parsley, salami and seasonings. Serve over pasta.

Scalloped Oysters

1/2 cup BUTTER
1/2 cup FLOUR
1 1/2 tsp. PAPRIKA
1/2 tsp. SALT
1/4 tsp. PEPPER
dash CAYENNE
1/2 clove GARLIC, minced
1 med. ONION, chopped
1/2 med. GREEN PEPPER, chopped
1 qt. FRESH OYSTERS
1 Tbsp. LEMON JUICE
2 tsp. WORCESTERSHIRE SAUCE
1/4 cup CRACKER CRUMBS

Preheat oven to 400 degrees; grease a 2 qt. casserole. Melt butter in large skillet over medium heat. Remove from heat, add flour and stir until smooth. Return to heat and cook, stirring constantly until brown (about 5 minutes). Add spices, garlic, onion and green pepper. Stir constantly and cook an additional 3 to 5 minutes. Add oysters, their juices, lemon juice and Worcestershire sauce; stir well. Pour into prepared casserole, sprinkle with cracker crumbs. Bake at 400 degrees for 20 minutes. Serves 6.

Roasted Oysters on the Half Shell

WHOLE OYSTERS, scrubbed
ROCK SALT or ALUMINUM FOIL
GRATED PARMESAN CHEESE
BLACK PEPPER
RAW BACON STRIPS, cut into pieces as desired

Using oyster knife, remove top shells from oysters, taking care to retain as much oyster liquor as possible. Arrange in shallow baking pan, using a bed of rock salt or crumpled foil to prop them up and keep them from losing their liquor. Sprinkle each oyster with 1/2 tsp. parmesan cheese, a dash of pepper and top with pieces of raw bacon. Bake at 400 degrees until bacon crisps, about 20 minutes.

Salmon Pot Pie

1 (16 oz. can) SALMON,
    drained, reserving liquid
1 cup CELERY, sliced
1 cup FROZEN PEAS
4 Tbsp. BUTTER
3 Tbsp. ONION, minced
6 Tbsp. FLOUR
1 1/2 cups MILK
1 tsp. SALT
dash PEPPER
1/8 tsp. PAPRIKA
1 Tbsp. LEMON JUICE
1 tsp. CHOPPED PARSLEY
BISCUIT DOUGH

Flake salmon; set aside. Cook celery and peas in boiling, salted water until tender; drain, reserving liquid. In medium sauce-pan, melt butter; add onion and sauté 2 minutes. Stir in flour until smooth. Combine reserved salmon liquid and vegetable liquid to measure 3/4 cup, and add to flour mixture with milk, stirring constantly. Cook until bubbly and thickened. Stir in remaining ingredients. Combine flaked salmon with cream sauce and vegetables. Turn mixture into large casserole. Prepare biscuit dough; roll 1/4 inch thick and cut in rounds. Place on top of salmon mixture and bake at 425 degrees about 12 minutes until thoroughly heated through and biscuits are brown.

Scallop Stir Fry

1 lb. SCALLOPS
3 Tbsp. COOKING OIL
1 clove GARLIC, minced
1/4 cup GREEN ONION, sliced
1 cup CELERY, diagonally cut
1 (8 oz. can) WATER CHESTNUTS, drained, sliced
1/4 lb. FRESH CHINESE PEA PODS, tips and strings removed
1 1/2 Tbsp. SOY SAUCE
1 Tbsp. COOKING SHERRY
1/2 cup CHICKEN STOCK, chilled
1 Tbsp. CORN STARCH
1 TOMATO, cut into thin wedges
4 cups HOT COOKED RICE

Rinse scallops in cool water; drain, pat dry and cut in half. In a wok or large skillet, cook scallops in hot oil for about 2 minutes, turning occasionally. Remove scallops from pan and set aside. To the skillet, add garlic and onion and stir fry for about 1 minute. Add celery, water chestnuts and pea pods. Cook and stir vegetables until hot, but still crisp (about 3 to 5 minutes). Combine soy sauce, sherry, chilled stock and corn starch. Pour mixture over vegetables and cook and stir until sauce is thickened and bubbly. Add scallops and tomato wedges, heat one minute. Serve over hot cooked rice.

Crab Casserole

1 cup FRESH CRAB, flaked
1 Tbsp. LEMON JUICE
1 can CREAM OF CHICKEN
   SOUP
3/4 cup MAYONNAISE
1 cup CELERY, chopped
1 Tbsp. ONION, grated
1/2 cup SLICED ALMONDS
1 tsp. SALT
1/2 tsp. PEPPER
3 HARD BOILED EGGS,
   peeled, sliced
2 cups CRUSHED POTATO
   CHIPS

Arrange crab in buttered casserole dish; sprinkle with lemon juice. Combine remaining ingredients in order listed, pour over crab and top with chips. Bake at 400 degrees for 20 minutes.

Windward Prawn Curry

Windward Inn — Florence

16 to 20 TIGER PRAWNS, peeled, cleaned
2 Tbsp. FLOUR
1 Tbsp. med. YELLOW CURRY
2 Tbsp. BUTTER
1/2 tsp. FRESH GARLIC, chopped
1 cup ONIONS, diced
1/2 cup GREEN PEPPERS, diced
1 cup FRESH MUSHROOMS, sliced
1 cup FRESH TOMATOES, diced
1/2 cup WHITE WINE

Coat prawns with flour and curry. Sauté in 12-inch pan with butter, heated until sizzling. Toss until lightly browned. Add garlic and all vegetables, except tomatoes. Gently stir until heated but still firm. Add tomatoes and wine, simmer for 3 minutes. Serve over rice or pasta. Serves 6.

If you're a bug, don't visit the Darlingtonia Botanical Wayside at Florence near Yachats. A half mile walkway leads through waving clumps of carnivorous, insect-catching cobra lilies. These lilies use a sweet scent to lure victims into their slippery, digestive-like, juice-filled interiors. Twelve miles to the north, Oregon's most powerful beacon shines forth from the Heceta Lighthouse.

Shrimp & Crab Au Gratin

3 Tbsp. BUTTER
1/4 cup FLOUR
1 1/4 cups MILK
1 tsp. DILL WEED
1/2 tsp. SALT
1/8 tsp. PEPPER
1 (6 oz. can) CRAB MEAT, drained
4 oz. FROZEN SHRIMP, thawed
12 SODA CRACKERS, crushed
1 cup CHEDDAR CHEESE, grated

Melt butter in heavy saucepan. Stir in flour until smooth and bubbly; gradually stir in milk. Bring to a boil, stirring constantly. Add seasonings, crab and shrimp. Pour into 4 individual buttered au gratin dishes and top with crackers and cheese. Bake in preheated 400 degree oven for 10 minutes until golden brown. Serves 4.

Shrimp & Rice Casserole

1 can MUSHROOM SOUP
1 Tbsp. ONION, chopped
2 Tbsp. GREEN PEPPER,
   chopped
2 Tbsp. MARGARINE
1 Tbsp. LEMON JUICE
1/2 tsp. DRY MUSTARD
1/2 tsp. WORCESTERSHIRE
   SAUCE
dash PEPPER
1/2 cup CHEESE, cubed
2 cups COOKED RICE
1/2 lb. COOKED SHRIMP
1/4 cup SLIVERED ALMONDS

Combine all ingredients except almonds, reserving a few shrimp for garnish. Spread mixture in baking dish; top with almonds and reserved shrimp. Bake at 375 degrees for 30 minutes. Serves 4.

Salmon Soufflé

1 (8 oz. can) SALMON
dash LEMON JUICE
1 can CREAM OF MUSHROOM SOUP
3 EGGS
1/2 cup CELERY, diced
1/2 cup ONION
1/4 cup GREEN PEPPER, diced
4 slices BREAD, dried in oven
1/2 lb. CHEESE, grated

Drain and flake salmon, reserving liquid. In a mixing bowl, combine reserved liquid, lemon juice, mushroom soup, eggs, celery, onion and green pepper. Break bread into pieces about the size of a postage stamp; combine with salmon and rest of ingredients. Place in greased casserole and bake at 325 degrees for 45 minutes or until knife comes out clean.

Tuna Casserole

1 lb. EGG NOODLES
2 Tbsp. BUTTER
1 Tbsp. DRY MUSTARD
1 Tbsp. FLOUR
1 (10 oz. can) EVAPORATED MILK
2 (7 oz. cans) TUNA, drained
10 oz. FROZEN MIXED VEGETABLES
1 1/2 cups CHEDDAR CHEESE, grated

Prepare noodles according to package directions. While they are cooking, melt butter in skillet; mix in mustard and flour to form a roux. Gradually add milk and whisk until it comes to a boil and thickens. Flake tuna with a fork; add vegetables, tuna, and one cup of grated cheese to the sauce. Turn into greased casserole and bake at 375 degrees for 40 minutes. Remove from oven, sprinkle with remaining cheese and bake 5 additional minutes. As an alternative, try substituting canned salmon, chopped spinach instead of mixed vegetables and fresh pasta instead of noodles.

Side Dishes

Baseball Beans

Bob Richmond, President, Northwest League Baseball — Eugene

2 cans RANCH BEANS
2 cans PORK AND BEANS
1 can KIDNEY BEANS
1 or 2 cans FRENCH STYLE GREEN
    BEANS
1 can GREEN CHILES, optional
1/2 bottle HOT CATSUP
1/2 cup BROWN SUGAR

Drain all but the ranch beans, add hot catsup and brown sugar. Bake uncovered for about an hour at 350 degrees.

According to Bob Richmond, "My wife fixes these a lot in the summer, as they are a good addition for a barbecue, and make a great dish to take to a potluck. They are very easy, and always 'A HIT'." Baseball fans will find their favorite pastime in Eugene, watching the Northwest League Emeralds each summer.

Broccoli Bake

1 pkg. FROZEN BROCCOLI CUTS
1 can CREAM OF MUSHROOM SOUP
1 (3 oz. pkg.) CREAM CHEESE

Cook broccoli according to directions; drain very well. Place in 1 1/2 qt. casserole; blend soup with cream cheese until smooth. Pour over broccoli; bake in 350 degree oven for 15 to 20 minutes. Serves 6.

Golden Onions

6 med. ONIONS, peeled, cut
   in half crosswise
2 Tbsp. MARGARINE, melted
2 Tbsp. CHILI SAUCE

2 Tbsp. HONEY
1 tsp. PAPRIKA
1/2 tsp. SALT
1/8 tsp. PEPPER

In a greased 12 x 8 x 2 baking dish, place onions cut side up. In small bowl, stir together margarine and remaining ingredients. Brush over onion halves; bake covered in 350 degree oven one hour, or until fork tender. Serves 6.

Squash Casserole

1 (10 oz. pkg.) FROZEN SQUASH
1 cup SHARP CHEESE, grated
2 EGGS, well beaten
1 can CREAM OF MUSHROOM SOUP
1/2 stick MARGARINE, melted
3 slices BREAD, cubed, including crust

Cook squash according to directions; drain. Place half of squash in greased 2 qt. casserole. Sprinkle half the grated cheese over squash. Combine beaten eggs and soup and pour half of this over the cheese. Repeat with another layer of squash, grated cheese and soup mix. Stir bread cubes in melted margarine and spoon over top of casserole. Bake in preheated oven at 300 degrees for one hour. (Try using broccoli instead of squash.)

Scalloped Corn

2 cans cut CORN
3 EGGS, beaten
1 cup MILK
1 1/2 tsp. SALT

1/8 tsp. PEPPER
2 Tbsp. BUTTER, melted
BUTTERED BREAD CRUMBS

Combine all ingredients, except bread crumbs. Mix well. Pour into buttered 1 1/2 quart casserole. Sprinkle with bread crumbs. Bake, uncovered, at 350 degrees for 90 minutes. Variations: Add 1 Tbsp. flour or cornstarch; add 1 Tbsp. minced onion.

Spinach Au Gratin

1 (15 oz. can) SPINACH
1/2 cup CHEESE, grated
3 tbsp. CREAM

SALT
PAPRIKA

Drain spinach and spread in shallow baking dish. Cover it with cheese and cream; sprinkle with salt and paprika. Place under broiler until cheese is melted. Serves 4.

Spinach Soufflé

2 (10 oz. pkgs.) FROZEN CHOPPED SPINACH
1/2 cup SOUR CREAM
1 to 2 Tbsp. ONION SOUP MIX
BUTTERED BREAD CRUMBS

Thaw and drain spinach; blend in sour cream to moisten. Stir in onion soup mix; top with buttered crumbs and bake at 350 degrees for 25 minutes. Serves 6.

Umatilla 'Zuiche' Casserole

Essie Nuzum — Umatilla

2 Tbsp. ONION, finely chopped
2 Tbsp. MARGARINE
1/4 cup SOUR CREAM
1/2 cup SHARP CHEDDAR CHEESE, grated
3 EGGS
1/2 tsp. SALT
dash NUTMEG
dash PEPPER
1 1/2 cups HALF AND HALF
2 or 3 med. ZUCCHINI, sliced, cooked, well drained
1/2 cup CRACKER CRUMBS

Sauté onion in margarine; when golden, remove pan from heat and stir in sour cream. Add cheese; return to low heat and stir until cheese melts. Beat eggs, spices and half and half together. Add to onion mixture. Place zucchini in a greased 2 1/2 qt. casserole. Pour onion mixture over zucchini; sprinkle crumbs over all. Bake 45 minutes to an hour in a 350 degree oven.

Best Ever Broccoli Casserole

1 (10 oz. pkg.) FROZEN CHOPPED BROCCOLI
1/2 cup SOUR CREAM
1/2 env. ONION SOUP MIX
1/2 cup CHEDDAR CHEESE, shredded

Cook broccoli according to directions; drain well and turn into baking dish. Add sour cream, soup mix and cheese; stir until mixed well. Bake at 350 degrees until cheese melts.

Spinach & Rice Casserole

1 pkg. FROZEN CHOPPED SPINACH
4 EGGS
3 cups cooked RICE
1 cup MILK
1 lb. CHEESE, grated
1/2 tsp. each THYME, ROSEMARY, MARJORAM
SALT and PEPPER to taste

Cook spinach and drain. Beat eggs and mix all ingredients together in a casserole dish. Cook uncovered in oven at 350 degrees for 45 minutes in a pan of hot water. Serves 8.

Portland is the largest city in Oregon. The second largest, Eugene, is often called "The Emerald Empire". An architectural masterpiece, the Hult Center, has drawn wide praise since it opened in 1982. You'll find 3,000 rhododendrons blooming each spring at Hendricks Park, and over 300 varieties of roses budding in the Riverside Owens Rose Garden.

Onion Casserole

4 med. ONIONS, peeled and thinly sliced
1 cup WATER
1 can CREAM OF MUSHROOM SOUP
1/2 cup MILK
1 (9 oz. pkg.) POTATO CHIPS, crumbled
1 cup CHEDDAR CHEESE, grated
PAPRIKA
PARSLEY

Simmer onions in water until almost tender, 5 to 8 minutes; drain. Combine soup with milk. In buttered 2 qt. casserole, layer onions, chips, cheese and soup mixture. Sprinkle with paprika; bake at 350 degrees for 30 minutes. Garnish with parsley. Serves 6.

Baked Potatoes & Shrimp

8 Tbsp. BUTTER
8 Tbsp. FLOUR
3 cups MILK
1/2 cup MEDIUM SHARP CHEESE, grated
1 cup GREEN PEPPER, chopped
4 Tbsp. WORCESTERSHIRE SAUCE
2 tsp. DRY MUSTARD
6 Tbsp. SHERRY
SALT to taste
2 cups sm. SHRIMP
6 BAKED POTATOES

Melt butter and stir in flour; cook for 5 minutes over low heat. Slowly add milk, stirring until thickened. Stir in cheese, green pepper, Worcestershire, mustard, sherry and salt. When cheese is melted, add shrimp. Split baked potatoes; top with shrimp sauce. There will be about 1/2 cup for each potato. Serves 6.

Green Beans & Mushrooms

2 cans GREEN BEANS
1 Tbsp. BUTTER
2 Tbsp. FLOUR
1/4 tsp. SALT
dash PEPPER
2 Tbsp. ONION, diced
1 (6 oz. can) SLICED MUSHROOMS
1 (5 oz. can) WATER CHESTNUTS, drained, chopped
1 cup SOUR CREAM
8 oz. SWISS CHEESE, grated
CORN FLAKES

Heat and drain green beans. Combine butter, flour, salt, pepper, onion, mushrooms, water chestnuts and sour cream. Mix lightly with beans; place in lightly greased casserole. Top with grated cheese; sprinkle with crushed corn flakes. Bake at 400 degrees until bubbly hot, about 20 minutes. Serves 8.

Corn Casserole

2 EGGS, beaten
1 cube MARGARINE, melted
1 can CREAM STYLE CORN
2 cans WHOLE KERNEL CORN, drained
1/2 pt. SOUR CREAM
1 pkg. JIFFY® CORN MUFFIN MIX

Combine beaten eggs with melted margarine; mix in remaining ingredients stirring until combined. Pour into greased 9 x 13 baking dish; bake at 350 degrees for 35 minutes.

Corn Pudding

3 EGGS
2 cups MILK
1/2 cup HALF AND HALF
1 Tbsp. SUGAR
1 tsp. SALT

2 cups CORN, cut from cob
or cream style
1/4 cup BREAD CRUMBS
2 Tbsp. BUTTER, melted

Preheat oven to 350; grease a 1 1/2 qt. casserole. Beat eggs until light and fluffy; add milk, cream, sugar and salt. Stir in corn, bread crumbs and butter, and place casserole in pan of boiling water. Bake at 350 degrees for 50 to 60 minutes, or until custard sets.

Creamy Potatoes

1 Tbsp. BUTTER
1 Tbsp. FLOUR
1 cup MILK
PEPPER to taste
1 (16 oz. can) WHOLE POTATOES, drained

Melt butter in pan, add flour stirring constantly to keep it creamy. Add milk slowly, stirring constantly to make sauce. Add pepper and potatoes, heat. A speedy one pan dish. Serves 3.

Breads

Oregon Nut Coffee Cake

1/2 cup **MARGARINE**
1/2 cup **SHORTENING**
2 **EGGS**
1 tsp. **VANILLA**
1 1/4 cups **SUGAR**
2 cups **FLOUR**
1/2 tsp. **SALT**
1 tsp. **BAKING POWDER**
1/2 tsp. **BAKING SODA**
1 cup **SOUR CREAM**
1/2 cup **OREGON NUTS**
1/4 cup **SUGAR**
2 tsp. **CINNAMON**

Cream together margarine and shortening. Add eggs, vanilla and sugar; mix together well. Slowly add combined dry ingredients; add sour cream last and stir in well. Place half of the mixture in angel food cake pan; sprinkle with half the nuts, sugar and cinnamon. Add rest of batter, then remaining nut mixture. Bake at 350 degrees for one hour.

Hazelnut Pear Muffins

Romeo Inn Bed & Breakfast — Ashland

2 cups FLOUR
1/2 tsp. SALT
1 tsp. BAKING SODA
1'/2 tsp. BAKING POWDER
3/4 cup BROWN SUGAR
2 EGGS
3/4 cup VEGETABLE OIL

1 tsp. VANILLA
1 1/2 cups SHREDDED PEAR
1 1/2 tsp. CINNAMON
1 tsp. GINGER
1/2 cup TOASTED
    HAZELNUTS, chopped

Mix together the flour, salt, baking soda and baking powder. Set aside. In a medium size bowl, lightly beat the eggs. Add brown sugar, vegetable oil, vanilla, pear, cinnamon and ginger. Add to flour mixture, together with nuts and stir just till blended. Spoon into greased muffin tins. Bake at 400 degrees for about 20 to 25 minutes till lightly browned and a toothpick inserted in the center comes out clean. Makes 12.

In Medford, "City of Pear Orchards", is one of the nation's largest direct mail marketing firms boasting 33,000 square feet of prize winning roses, tulips, daffo-dils and dahlias.

Pear Raspberry Jam

Verna Smith — Bonanza

6 or 7 RIPE PEARS
1 (10 oz. pkg.) FROZEN RASPBERRIES, thawed
1/2 cup LEMON JUICE
6 cups SUGAR
1/2 bottle FRUIT PECTIN

Peel and finely chop pears. Measure raspberries and add pears to make 4 cups. Place in large pan, add lemon and sugar. Mix well; place over high heat. Bring to a full rolling boil; boil hard for one minute, stirring constantly. Remove from heat at once; stir in pectin and skim off foam. Stir and skim for about 5 minutes. Ladle quickly into glass containers; seal at once. Fills about 10 medium glass jars.

Hazelnut Biscotti

Chetco River Inn — Brookings

6 EGGS
2 cups SUGAR
1 Tbsp. BAKING POWDER
3 Tbsp. ANISE SEED
1 cup HAZELNUTS, finely chopped
2 tsp. ANISE FLAVORING

2 cubes BUTTER, melted,
   cooled
4 Tbsp. SHERRY
4 Tbsp. WATER
5 1/2 cups FLOUR

Blend all ingredients; dough will be sticky. Pat into 4 long logs 1/2 inch thick. Place 2 logs to a cookie sheet; bake at 375 degrees for 20 minutes until golden brown. Cool; cut into 1/2 to 3/4 inch slices. Lay slices flat on cookie sheet and bake 15 minutes more. Makes about 9 dozen, and they keep well.

> *Large groves of myrtlewood stand just east of Coos Bay and north of Brookings, where many roadside signs remind the traveler that you are in myrtlewood country. This distinctive hardwood is carved into dishes, jewelry and other items for sale at local stands. It takes over a century for the tree to grow large enough to be used. These trees have been known to reach 150 feet in height. Myrtlewood logs will not float.*

"Best-Ever" Rolls

2 EGGS
1 cup SUGAR
2 pkgs. DRY YEAST
1/4 cup WARM WATER

3/4 cup SHORTENING, melted
2 cups MILK, scalded
1 tsp. SALT
7 cups FLOUR

Beat the eggs and sugar together. Mix yeast with water and then combine with sugar and eggs. Blend melted shortening, milk and salt and stir into the combined mixture. Add flour until mixture is thoroughly combined. Place in greased bowl and cover with towel. Set in refrigerator until ready to form into rolls. About 2 hours before baking, remove dough and shape into desired rolls. Bake at 350 degrees, 15-20 minutes.

Vicki's Rhubarb Muffins

Vicki Lamb, Iris Inn — Ashland

1/2 cup BROWN SUGAR
1/2 cup SALAD OIL
1 EGG
2 tsp. VANILLA
1 cup BUTTERMILK
1 1/2 cups RHUBARB, diced

1/2 cup OREGON NUTS
2 1/2 cups FLOUR
1 tsp. BAKING SODA
1 tsp. BAKING POWDER
1/2 tsp. SALT

Combine first 5 ingredients; beat well with spoon. Stir in rhubarb and nuts. Combine last 4 ingredients and stir into rhubarb mixture. Spoon batter into muffin cups and bake at 400 degrees for 15 to 20 minutes. Makes 24 muffins.

Oregon's Nut & Fruit Bread

1/2 cup BUTTER, softened
3/4 cup SUGAR
2 EGGS
1/3 cup SOUR CREAM
1/4 cup ORANGE JUICE

zest of 2 ORANGES
1 3/4 cup FLOUR
1 1/2 tsp. BAKING POWDER
1 1/2 cup OREGON NUTS,
   chopped

Beat together first five ingredients. Combine the rest and add to the mixture. Do not overmix. Grease and flour 9 x 5 inch loaf pan and bake at 325 degrees for 45 to 50 minutes. Top with the following glaze:

Glaze:
2 Tbsp. CREAM
3/4 cup POWDERED SUGAR
1 Tbsp. ORANGE ZEST

Mix all ingredients well and spread over warm bread.

Fruit & Vegetable Muffins

4 cups ALL PURPOSE FLOUR
2 cups SUGAR
1 Tbsp. plus 1 tsp. BAKING SODA
1 heaping Tbsp. CINNAMON
1/2 tsp. NUTMEG
1 tsp. SALT
1/2 cup RAISINS
1/2 cup DATES, chopped
4 cups CARROTS, peeled, grated
2 lg. TART APPLES, peeled, cored, grated
1 cup ALMONDS, sliced
1 cup COCONUT, shredded
6 EGGS
1 1/3 cup VEGETABLE OIL
1 Tbsp. plus 1 tsp. VANILLA
1 Tbsp. ORANGE RIND, grated

Grease muffin tins; sift the flour, sugar, baking soda, cinnamon, nutmeg and salt in a bowl. Stir in the raisins, dates, carrots, apples, almonds and coconut. Beat the eggs with the oil, vanilla and orange rind and stir this mixture into the flour mixture until just combined. Fill muffin tins 2/3 full and bake in 350 degree oven about 20 minutes. Cool slightly before removing from the pans. Serve at room temperature. Yields 36.

Mashed Potato Biscuits

1 pkg. DRY YEAST
1/4 cup WARM WATER
1 cup MASHED POTATOES
1/2 cup SUGAR
1/2 cup SHORTENING
1 pt. MILK, boiling
FLOUR to thicken batter
1 tsp. BAKING POWDER
1 tsp. BAKING SODA
1 tsp. SALT
FLOUR to make light roll

Dissolve yeast in warm water and set aside. In a large bowl, add potatoes, sugar and shortening. Pour boiling milk over mixture and cool to lukewarm. Add yeast mixture, then enough flour to make a thin batter. Let rise 30 to 40 minutes; add baking powder, baking soda, salt and enough more flour to make a light roll mixture. Place in greased bowl, and grease top of the dough. Cover with foil and refrigerate. When you are ready to use, shape as desired, and bake at 350 degrees for 20 to 30 minutes.

Raspberry Tart Coffee Cake

Sea Quest Bed & Breakfast — Yachats

2 1/3 cups FLOUR
3/4 cup SUGAR
1/2 tsp. BAKING POWDER
1/2 tsp. BAKING SODA
1/8 tsp. SALT
3/4 cup BUTTER or MARGARINE
1 EGG, lightly beaten
3/4 cup BUTTERMILK
1/2 cup RASPBERRY PRESERVES

Grease and flour a 9 x 2 inch round tart pan with a removable bottom. In a large bowl, stir together dry ingredients. Using a pastry blender, cut in butter until mixture resembles coarse crumbs. Make a well in the center of dry ingredients. In a small bowl, combine egg and buttermilk. Pour egg mixture into dry ingredients and stir until moistened. Spread batter evenly in bottom of tart pan. Spread raspberry preserves over dough, leaving a 1 1/2 inch border. Bake in 350 degree oven 30 to 35 minutes until toothpick inserted in center comes out clean. Cool on a rack in the pan. Before serving, remove from pan and drizzle with glaze (see below). Serves 8 to 10.

Glaze:
    1 1/2 cups sifted powdered sugar
    2 to 3 Tbsp. lemon juice

> *Yachats (pronounced YAH-hahts) is a haven for anglers where smelt come to shore to spawn. Just south of town is the highest point on the Oregon coast, Cape Perpetua, offering a sweeping ocean view from its 800 foot headland. Sea Lion Caves is the only year round mainland home for sea lions.* **Sea Quest Bed & Breakfast** *is seated on a 2 1/2 acre bluff overlooking the outlet of 10 Mile Creek near Cape Perpetua.*

Amish Friendship Bread Starter

1/3 cup WARM WATER
2 pkgs. DRY YEAST
1 cup SUGAR
2 cups MILK
2 cups FLOUR

Pour water into bowl; sprinkle with yeast and 1 tsp. sugar. Let stand in warm place until double in size, about 10 minutes. In separate large bowl, combine milk, remaining sugar, flour and yeast mixture. Stir with wooden spoon until smooth. Cover loosely and allow to double or triple in size. Let stand overnight in warm place. Next day, stir mixture; cover loosely and refrigerate. Daily directions follow:

Day 1: Do nothing.

Days 2, 3, 4: Stir.

Day 5: Add **1 cup** each **FLOUR, SUGAR** and **MILK**. Stir together and place in large covered container, (this mixture grows.)

Days 6, 7, 8, 9: Stir.

Day 10: Add **1 cup** each **FLOUR, SUGAR** and **MILK.** Stir with wooden spoon until smooth. Pour one cup of mixture into each of three small containers. Keep one starter for yourself, and give the other two to friends.

To the remaining mixture, add:

2/3 cup OIL	**1 cup NUTS, chopped**
1/2 tsp. SALT	**1 sm. box INSTANT VANILLA**
2 cups FLOUR	**PUDDING**
1/2 tsp. BAKING SODA	**1 tsp. VANILLA**
1 1/4 tsp. BAKING POWDER	**1 cup SUGAR**
1 tsp. CINNAMON	**1 cup RAISINS**
3 EGGS	**1 cup CHOPPED DATES**

Mix well and pour into two well greased and sugared loaf pans, or one tube or bundt pan. Bake at 350 degrees for 40 to 50 minutes. Cool 10 minutes before removing from pan.

Pumpkin Muffins

Muffins:
- 2 1/4 cups FLOUR
- 1 tsp. BAKING SODA
- 1/2 tsp. SALT
- 1 1/2 tsp. CINNAMON
- 1/2 tsp. CORRIANDER
- 2 EGGS, lightly beaten
- 2 cups SUGAR
- 1 cup PUMPKIN
- 1/2 cup OIL
- 1/2 tsp. VANILLA

Filling:
- 6 oz. CREAM CHEESE, softened
- 1 EGG
- 1 Tbsp. SUGAR

Topping:
- 3/4 cup FLAKED COCONUT
- 1/2 cup PECANS, chopped
- 1/4 cup SUGAR
- 1/2 tsp. CINNAMON

In large bowl, combine flour, baking soda, salt, cinnamon and corriander. Set aside. In small bowl, combine eggs, sugar, pumpkin, oil and vanilla; mix well. Add liquid ingredients to dry ingredients and stir just until moistened. For filling: In small bowl, combine cream cheese, egg and sugar; mix well. For topping: In small bowl, combine coconut, pecans, sugar and cinnamon. To assemble, spoon half of batter into 24 greased or paper lined muffin cups, filling half full. Spoon cream cheese mixture evenly over partially filled muffin cups. Spoon remaining batter over cream cheese, carefully spreading to the edges. Sprinkle pecan topping over muffins, bake in preheated 350 degree oven for 20 to 25 minutes or until toothpick comes out clean. Cool in pan 3 to 4 minutes, remove from pan and cool on wire rack.

Bonanza Corn Bread

Pam Smith — Bonanza

- 1 cup FLOUR, sifted
- 1 Tbsp. SUGAR
- 1/2 tsp. SALT
- 2 tsp. BAKING POWDER
- 1 EGG
- 2 1/2 cups WHOLE KERNEL CORN
- 1/2 cup CHEESE, grated
- 1/4 cup BUTTER, melted

Combine sifted dry ingredients. Beat egg, add corn, cheese and butter. Combine with dry ingredients and bake at 400 degrees in a greased 8 x 8 x 2 inch pan for 35 minutes. Serves 6. (Add one cup of raisins, if desired.)

Aunt Bobbie's Sticky Bun Cake

Floras Lake House Bed & Breakfast — Langlois

CHOPPED NUTS (pecans or walnuts)
1 pkg. RHODES® FROZEN TEXAS or DINNER ROLLS
1 pkg. BUTTERSCOTCH PUDDING MIX (not instant)
1/4 cup melted BUTTER or MARGARINE
1/2 cup packed BROWN SUGAR
CINNAMON

Grease a Bundt cake pan, sprinkle chopped nuts over the bottom. Layer frozen rolls on top (1/2 pkg. or about 12 to 14 rolls). Dump dry pudding mix around on the top of rolls. Mix together the butter and sugar, pour on top. Sprinkle rolls with loads of cinnamon. Let raise overnight in cold oven, or covered on the counter. In morning, bake in preheated 350 degree oven for 18 to 20 minutes. Let cool about 5 minutes, and dump upside down onto plate. Enjoy!

Only a sand dune separates Floras Lake from the ocean. In 1910, about 400 people moved here on a promise of a canal being built linking the ocean and the lake. Everyone left after it was determined that a canal would drain the lake, since it was higher than the ocean. Today, Floras Lake is best known for its wind surfing.

Grandma's Brown Sugar Rolls

Barbara Roberts, former Governor of Oregon

1 3/4 cup FLOUR
1/3 cup SHORTENING
2 1/2 tsp. BAKING POWDER
3/4 tsp. SALT
3/4 cup MILK, approx.
BROWN SUGAR

Blend dry ingredients and shortening until mixture resembles fine crumbs. Stir in just enough milk so that dough leaves sides of bowl and rounds into a ball. Turn dough onto lightly floured surface and knead gently ten times. Roll out on lightly floured surface to 1/4 to 1/2 inch. Spread with butter or margarine and sprinkle with brown sugar. Roll up and cut into one-inch slices. Place sliced rolls, cut side down, on lightly greased baking sheet or dish, and bake at 350 degrees approximately 30 minutes until lightly brown. Do not overcook.

"My Grandma was a wonderful cook. Although she seldom measured anything...every dish she prepared was a treat. Grandma's rolls were always served hot and with lots of love," Gov. Roberts says. *"I hope you, too, will enjoy serving our family's favorite the same way."*

Founded in 1841 by missionary Jason Lee, Salem is home to Williamette University, the oldest university west of Missouri. Antique woolen mills, historic homes, and wineries are attractions in this capital city of over 100,000 residents.

Blueberry Buckle

Chick-a-dee Blueberry Nursery — Sherwood

1/2 cup SHORTENING	1/2 cup MILK
3/4 cup SUGAR	2 cups FRESH BLUEBERRIES
1 EGG	1/2 cup SUGAR
2 cups FLOUR	1/2 cup FLOUR
2 1/2 tsp. BAKING POWDER	1/2 tsp. CINNAMON
1/4 tsp. SALT	1/4 cup MARGARINE

Thoroughly cream shortening and sugar; add egg and beat until light and fluffy. Sift together 2 cups flour, baking powder and salt. Add to creamed mixture, alternately with milk. Spread in greased 11 x 7 x 2 pan; top with berries. Mix remaining sugar, flour and cinnamon. Cut in margarine until crumbly and sprinkle over berries. Bake at 350 degrees for 45 minutes. Cut in squares and serve warm with ice cream or sweetened whipped cream.

Lemon Sour Cream Pie

Lord Bennett's Restaurant & Lounge — Bandon-by-the-Sea

1 cup SUGAR
3 1/2 Tbsp. CORN STARCH
1 Tbsp. LEMON RIND, grated
1/2 cup fresh LEMON JUICE
3 EGG YOLKS, slightly beaten
1 cup MILK

1/4 cup BUTTER
1 cup SOUR CREAM
1 baked (9 in.) PIE SHELL
1 cup WHIPPING CREAM,
  whipped

Combine sugar, corn starch, lemon rind, juice, yolks and milk in a heavy saucepan. Cook over medium heat till thick. Stir in butter and cool mixture to room temperature or cooler. Stir in sour cream and pour filling into baked shell. Cover with whipped cream and garnish with lemon twists. Refrigerate.

*The spectacular view from the expansive dining room at the **Lord Bennett** provides a great place to enjoy the "Storm Watching Capital of the World", Bandon-by-the-Sea, where cheese making and cranberry growing are king. Unique cranberry candies are produced in a sweet shop in the Old Town district. A tour through the cheese factory will reward you with a delectable curd to tantalize your taste buds.*

Pumpkin Ice Cream Pie

Annette Wilkins — Sherwood

1/4 cup BROWN SUGAR
3/4 cup PUMPKIN
1/2 tsp. CINNAMON
1/4 tsp. GINGER
dash NUTMEG
dash CLOVES

1/4 tsp. SALT
1 qt. VANILLA ICE CREAM,
  softened
1 GRAHAM CRACKER CRUST
WHIPPED CREAM

Bring to a boil first 7 ingredients, stirring constantly. Cool, refrigerate until mixture begins to mound. Then, beat into ice cream; spread into pastry shell and freeze. Serve with whipped cream. This is refreshing after a big holiday meal.

Apple Squares

1 cup FLOUR
1/2 cup SHORTENING
1/2 cup BROWN SUGAR
1/2 tsp. BAKING SODA
1/2 tsp. SALT
1 cup QUICK OATS
2 1/2 cups APPLES, sliced
2 Tbsp. MARGARINE
1/2 cup SUGAR

Cut flour into shortening, brown sugar, baking soda, salt and oats. Blend until crumbly; spread half of mixture into 8 x 8 or 9 x 9 cake pan. Combine apples, margarine and sugar; arrange on crumb mixture and top with remaining crumbs. Bake in 350 degree oven for 40 to 45 minutes. Serves 8.

Just east of Portland, Hood River has dubbed itself, "The Apple Center of Oregon". You can watch processing and packaging of fresh fruit at the growers' cooperative plant during the harvest season. The city is only a few minutes from Bonneville Dam and Multnomah Falls, the nation's second highest waterfall. East along the Columbia, The Dalles marked the end of the Oregon Trail in the mid 1840s. At Seufert Park, board a train for a free ride to The Dalles Dam.

Mayonnaise Cake

1 cup OREGON NUTS, chopped
1 cup DATES, chopped
1 tsp. BAKING SODA
1 cup HOT WATER
2 cups FLOUR, sifted
3/4 tsp. SALT
1 tsp. BAKING POWDER
1 cup SUGAR
3 Tbsp. COCOA
1 tsp. VANILLA
1 cup MAYONNAISE

Combine first 4 ingredients together; let cool. Mix dry ingredients and add to cooled mixture. Beat until smooth. Add vanilla and fold in mayonnaise. Bake in 325 degree oven for about an hour. May bake in angel food cake pan, if desired.

Brownie Pudding

1 cup FLOUR
1/2 cup SUGAR
2 tsp. BAKING POWDER
1/4 tsp. SALT
1/2 cup COCOA, divided
1/2 cup MILK

2 Tbsp. MARGARINE, melted
1 tsp. VANILLA
1/2 cup CHOCOLATE CHIPS
1/2 cup BROWN SUGAR, firmly
   packed
1 3/4 cup BOILING WATER

Preheat oven to 350 degrees; combine flour, sugar, baking powder, salt and 1/4 cup cocoa in a bowl. Stir in milk, margarine and vanilla until smooth. Stir in chocolate chips; spread in ungreased, shallow 1 1/2 qt. casserole. Sprinkle brown sugar and remaining cocoa on top. Place in oven; pour boiling water over top. Bake 35 minutes; cool 10 minutes before serving. As the cake bakes, a gooey pudding forms on the bottom - like magic! Serve with ice cream, if desired. Serves 6.

Earthquake Cake

1 sm. can COCONUT
1 cup OREGON NUTS, your choice, coarsely chopped
1 GERMAN CHOCOLATE CAKE MIX
1 (8 oz. pkg.) CREAM CHEESE
1 cube MARGARINE
1 lb. POWDERED SUGAR
1 tsp. VANILLA

Grease bottom only of a 9 x 13 pan. Place coconut and nuts in pan; mix cake as directed and pour over nuts and coconut. Combine cream cheese, margarine, powdered sugar and vanilla. Spoon over cake mix. Bake at 325 degrees for 45 to 60 minutes.

Speaking of earthquakes, it was in 1993 that considerable damage was done in the Mt. Angel region. Mt. Angel boasts a German-Swiss heritage, and is home to one of the most popular folk festivals, "Oktoberfest". Mt. Angel Abbey, a monastery established by Benedictine monks from Switzerland, was heavily damaged by the quake.

Chocolate Peanut Butter Pie

3 EGGS
1 cup CORN SYRUP
1/2 cup SUGAR
1/3 cup CRUNCHY PEANUT
    BUTTER

1/2 tsp. VANILLA
1/2 cup CHOCOLATE CHIPS
1 (9 in. unbaked) PIE SHELL
WHIPPED CREAM
PEANUTS, for garnish

In a mixing bowl, beat eggs and stir in corn syrup, sugar, peanut butter and vanilla. Mix well. Sprinkle chocolate chips over bottom of pie crust; pour filling over chips. Bake at 375 degrees for 20 minutes. Garnish with whipped cream, peanuts and more chocolate chips, if desired. Test for doneness as you would with pecan pie.

Ice Cream Pie

1 qt. VANILLA ICE CREAM, softened
1 (6 oz. can) FROZEN LEMONADE
1 (9 in.) GRAHAM CRACKER CRUST

Add frozen concentrate to the softened ice cream. Mix with electric beater on low until well mixed and smooth. Pour into prepared crust and refreeze.

Yummy Ice Cream Dessert

3/4 cube BUTTER
1 (1 lb. pkg.) OREOS®, crushed
1/2 gal. VANILLA ICE CREAM,
    softened

FUDGE SAUCE
8 oz. WHIPPED TOPPING

Melt butter and combine with cookies and place in 9 x 13 pan. Soften ice cream until proper consistency to spread over cookies. Place in freezer until firm. Spread desired amount of fudge sauce over ice cream; freeze again. Top with whipped topping; sprinkle with more crushed cookies. As an option, layer bananas.

Caramel Pudding Cake

1/2 cup MARGARINE, softened
1/2 cup SUGAR
1 1/2 cups FLOUR
1 tsp. BAKING POWDER
1/2 tsp. SALT

1/2 cup MILK
1/2 cup RAISINS, optional
1 cup BROWN SUGAR, packed
2 cups COLD WATER

In a mixing bowl, cream margarine and sugar. Combine flour, baking powder and salt; add to creamed mixture with milk. Stir until smooth. Stir in raisins; spread in greased 8-inch square baking pan. Combine brown sugar in cold water, pour over batter. Bake at 350 degrees 40 minutes or until golden brown. Serve warm. Serves 9.

Apple Strudel

1/2 cup MILK, scalded
6 Tbsp. SUGAR
3/4 tsp. SALT
3 Tbsp. BUTTER
4 1/2 tsp. YEAST
6 Tbsp. WATER
1 EGG, well beaten
2 cups FLOUR
2 cups APPLES, sliced

Topping:
   3 Tbsp. BROWN SUGAR
   1/2 tsp. CINNAMON
   1/2 tsp. NUTMEG
   3 Tbsp. BUTTER, melted

To the scalded milk, add sugar, salt and butter. Cool to lukewarm; combine yeast with water and add egg combining with milk mixture. Stir in flour, place in greased 9 x 13 pan. Spread apples over dough; sprinkle with combined brown sugar, cinnamon and nutmeg. Drizzle with melted butter. Let rise in warm place 40 minutes. Bake at 400 degrees for 25 minutes; then frost.

Coconut Macaroon Pie

1 1/2 cups SUGAR
1/2 tsp. SALT
2 EGGS
1/2 cup MARGARINE
1/4 cup FLOUR

1/2 cup MILK
1 1/2 cups SHREDDED
   COCONUT, divided
1 (9 in. unbaked) PIE SHELL

    Beat sugar, salt and eggs until mixture is lemon colored. Add margarine and flour, blending well. Add milk and one cup of coconut. Pour into pie shell; top with remaining coconut. Bake in slow oven 325 degrees for about an hour.

Chocolate Peanut Crunch

1 cup FLOUR
1/2 tsp. BAKING SODA
1/3 cup MARGARINE, melted
1/3 cup SUGAR
1/3 cup BROWN SUGAR

1 EGG
1/2 tsp. VANILLA
1/2 cup PEANUT BUTTER
1/4 cup CHOCOLATE
   FLAVORED SYRUP

    In small bowl, combine flour and soda; set aside. On medium speed of mixer, beat margarine and sugars until light and fluffy. Add egg and vanilla; beat well. Add peanut butter and chocolate syrup and continue to mix until well mixed. Add flour and soda in several additions, beating after each addition. Bake at 375 degrees for 10 minutes, remove from oven and let stand one minute. Remove to rack to cool.

Scalloped Rhubarb

1 cube MARGARINE, melted
3 cups STALE BREAD, cubed, no crust
2 cups RHUBARB, diced

1 cup SUGAR
RED FOOD COLOR,
   as needed

    In greased 9 x 13 pan, combine margarine with bread cubes; mix well. Add rhubarb and sugar, mixing well. Use food color to obtain desired coloring. Add 1 Tbsp. water in each corner of the pan. Bake 45 minutes at 325 degrees.

Pecan Tea Cakes

1/2 cup MARGARINE
1 (3 oz. pkg.) CREAM CHEESE, softened
1 cup FLOUR
1 EGG, beaten
3/4 cup BROWN SUGAR, packed
1 Tbsp. MARGARINE, melted
1 tsp. VANILLA
1/2 tsp. ALMOND EXTRACT
1 cup PECANS, chopped

In small mixer bowl, beat margarine and cream cheese; add flour and beat well. Cover and chill about one hour. Divide chilled dough into 24 portions; roll each into 3-inch circle. Fit into 1 3/4 inch muffin cups, flute to fit. In a small mixing bowl, combine egg, brown sugar, margarine, vanilla, almond and pecans. Pour filling into prepared muffin cups; bake at 375 degrees for 15 to 18 minutes.

Lemon Cream Dessert

1 1/2 cups FLOUR
1/4 cup SUGAR
1/2 cup MARGARINE
10 oz. CREAM CHEESE, softened
1 pkg. LEMON PUDDING, cooked as directed
2 cups POWDERED SUGAR
5 1/2 cups FROZEN WHIPPED TOPPING, thawed, divided

In mixing bowl combine flour, sugar and margarine, mixing until crumbly. Press into bottom of 9 x 13 baking pan and bake at 325 degrees for 15 minutes. Remove from oven and cool thoroughly. Combine cream cheese, powdered sugar and 2 1/2 cups whipped topping and mix on medium speed with electric mixer until uniformly blended. Spread evenly over cooled crust. Spread lemon pudding evenly over cream cheese mixture. Spread remaining whipped topping over the pudding. Cover pan and chill until firm, preferably overnight.

Fruit Cobbler

5 cups MIXED OREGON FRUIT

Batter:
   3/4 cup SUGAR
   1/8 tsp. SALT
   1 tsp. BAKING POWDER
   1/2 cup MARGARINE
   1 cup FLOUR
   1/2 cup MILK

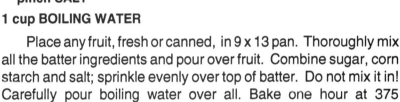

Topping:
   1 cup SUGAR
   1 Tbsp. CORN STARCH
   pinch SALT

1 cup BOILING WATER

Place any fruit, fresh or canned, in 9 x 13 pan. Thoroughly mix all the batter ingredients and pour over fruit. Combine sugar, corn starch and salt; sprinkle evenly over top of batter. Do not mix it in! Carefully pour boiling water over all. Bake one hour at 375 degrees.

Pumpkin Ginger Snap Pie

1 1/2 cups HALF AND HALF, cold
1 lg. pkg. VANILLA INSTANT PUDDING
1 (8 oz. ctn.) NON DAIRY WHIPPED TOPPING
1 cup OREGON NUTS, chopped
1 cup GINGER SNAPS, chopped
1/2 cup CANNED PUMPKIN
1 1/2 Tbsp. PUMPKIN PIE SPICE
1 (8 inch) GRAHAM CRACKER PIE CRUST

Pour cream in bowl; add pudding and pie filling mix. Beat with wire whip until blended, about one minute. Let stand 5 minutes; fold in whipped topping, nuts, ginger snaps, pumpkin and spices. Place in crust; freeze until firm, about 6 hours. Remove from freezer and let stand 10 minutes before serving. You may also place pie in refrigerator to set up.

Delicious Pumpkin Chiffon Pie

1 env. UNFLAVORED GELATIN
1/4 cup COLD WATER
3 EGGS, separated
1/2 cup SUGAR
1/2 cup PUMPKIN

1/2 cup MILK
1/2 tsp. each GINGER, SALT,
  CINNAMON, NUTMEG
1/2 cup SUGAR
WHIPPED CREAM

Dissolve gelatin in cold water; set aside. In saucepan, beat egg yolks slightly; add sugar, pumpkin, milk and spices. Cook until thick; add gelatin to hot mixture and cool. Beat egg whites and sugar (as you would for meringue) and fold into cooled mixture. Pour into baked 9 1/2 or 10-inch pie shell; serve with whipped cream.

Elegant Chocolate Mousse

4 oz. GERMANS® SWEET CHOCOLATE
4 EGGS, separated
1/2 cube BUTTER

dash SALT
1 tsp. VANILLA
6 Tbsp. SUGAR

Place chocolate into a saucepan; cover with 2 inches of very hot water. Cover with lid; let stand about 5 minutes. When you can stick your finger through the chocolate, it is soft enough to complete the recipe. When soft, but not dissolved, drain off water. Add egg yolks; stir with whisk and cook over very low heat until thick. Remove from heat; add butter, salt and vanilla. Mix well. Cool, but do not let it get cold. Beat egg whites adding sugar gradually when the whites are soft peaks. Continue beating until meringue is very stiff. Beat some of the whites into chocolate, mixing well. Fold remainder of whites into chocolate; pour into individual serving dishes. Cover with plastic wrap, and refrigerate until ready to serve. Decorate with whipped cream and chocolate shavings. Serves 6.

Chocolate Chip Pie

1/2 cup MARGARINE
1/4 cup BROWN SUGAR
1/4 cup SUGAR
1 tsp. VANILLA
2 EGGS
1/4 cup FLOUR

1/2 cup NUTS, chopped, optional
1 cup MINIATURE CHOCOLATE CHIPS
1 (9 inch unbaked) PIE SHELL

Melt margarine, turn into mixing bowl and add sugars, vanilla and eggs, blending thoroughly. Add flour and nuts; mix. Continue whipping until mixture is light in color. Stir in chocolate chips and pour into pie shell. Bake at 325 degrees for 1 1/2 hours. Use toothpick to check filling. Bake another 15 minutes, if necessary. If pie browns too quickly, cover with foil to prevent burning.

Hazelnut Chocolate Chip Cookies

2 1/3 cups FLOUR
1 tsp. BAKING POWDER
1/2 tsp. SALT
1/2 cup SUGAR
1 cup BROWN SUGAR
1 cup MARGARINE, softened

2 EGGS
1 cup CHOCOLATE CHIPS
3/4 cup OREGON HAZELNUTS, chopped
1 tsp. VANILLA

Combine flour, baking powder and salt; set aside. In large bowl, cream sugars with margarine for 3 minutes. Add eggs, one at a time, beating well after each addition. Stir dry ingredients into batter, folding in chocolate chips, hazelnuts and vanilla. Drop by teaspoonful onto greased sheet. Flatten gently with fork. Bake at 350 degrees for 10 to 12 minutes.

Southern Oregon has many English walnut and hazelnut orchards. They are ready for harvest in October. You can gather fallen nuts, and pay by the pound. To dry nuts place in mesh sacks.

Biscuit Dessert

1 can FRUIT, undrained
1 cup SUGAR
2 Tbsp. FLOUR
1 can REFRIGERATED BISCUITS
MARGARINE, melted
1/2 cup SUGAR
CINNAMON

Bring fruit to a boil and pour in baking dish. Combine flour and sugar; place evenly on top of fruit. Place biscuits on top of fruit, using a tablespoon of margarine on top of each. Spread evenly with sugar; sprinkle with cinnamon. Bake at 350 degrees for 20 to 30 minutes. If you use peaches, almond flavoring is good.

Apple Bread Pudding

8 slices BREAD
1 1/2 to 2 lbs. COOKING
   APPLES
1/2 cup GOLDEN RAISINS
1 1/3 cups MILK
1/4 cup MARGARINE
5 EGGS, beaten

1/2 cup SUGAR
1/2 tsp. GROUND CINNAMON
1/4 tsp. GROUND NUTMEG
1/4 tsp. SALT
1/4 cup BROWN SUGAR,
   packed

Toast bread lightly and cut diagonally into fourths. Arrange a single layer of bread in bottom of buttered (11 3/4 x 7 1/2 x 2-inch) baking dish. Core and slice one apple. Core and diced enough of remaining apples to measure 4 cups. Spread diced apples evenly on bread. Sprinkle raisins over apples. Arrange remaining bread in two lengthwise rows on diced apples. Place apple slices between rows of bread. Heat milk and margarine only until margarine melts. Combine eggs, sugar, spices and salt. Gradually add milk, stirring constantly. Pour over bread and apples; sprinkle with brown sugar. Bake uncovered 40 to 45 minutes (or until set) at 350 degrees. Serve warm or cold, topping with sour cream, if desired.

Pineapple Cream Pie

2 Tbsp CORNSTARCH
3/4 cup SUGAR, divided
1/2 tsp. SALT
2 1/4 cups CRUSHED PINEAPPLE, undrained
2 EGGS, separated
1 Tbsp. LEMON JUICE
1 (8 in.) PIE SHELL, baked

In saucepan, combine cornstarch, 1/4 cup sugar and salt, add pineapple and cook, stirring constantly, until mixture is clear and thick. Beat egg yolks with 1/4 cup sugar, add to pineapple mixture and cook one minute. Remove from heat and cool, then stir in lemon juice and pour into cold pie shell. Top with meringue made with egg whites and remaining 1/4 cup sugar. Bake at 300 degrees for 30 minutes. Remove from oven and cool, then refrigerate.

Chocolate Cherry Ring

2 cups FLOUR
1 tsp. BAKING SODA
1/8 tsp. SALT
3/4 cup SUGAR
1 tsp. CINNAMON
2 EGGS, beaten
1/2 cup OIL
2 tsp. VANILLA
1 (21 oz. can) CHERRY PIE FILLING
1 cup CHOCOLATE CHIPS
1 cup NUTS, chopped
POWDERED SUGAR

In large bowl, stir together flour, soda, salt, sugar and cinnamon. In another bowl, combine eggs, oil and vanilla. Add to flour mixture; mix well. Stir in pie filling, chocolate chips and nuts. Turn batter into greased and floured 10-inch Bundt pan. Bake at 350 degrees, until done, 45 minutes to one hour. Cool on rack 15 minutes; remove from pan and cool. Sift powdered sugar on top. If cake is wrapped airtight, it freezes well.

Caramel Crunch Pie

2 cups GRAHAM CRACKER CRUMBS
3 Tbsp. plus 1/4 cup PEANUTS, chopped, divided
6 Tbsp. MARGARINE, melted
2 (8 oz. pkgs.) CREAM CHEESE, softened
1/3 cup plus 1 Tbsp. BROWN SUGAR, divided
1/4 cup CORN SYRUP
2 Tbsp. CORN STARCH
3 EGGS
1/3 cup plus 1/4 cup SOUR CREAM, divided
1 1/4 tsp. VANILLA
6 (2.07 oz. ea.) SNICKERS® CANDY BARS, coarsely chopped
3/4 cup MILK CHOCOLATE CHIPS, melted
1/4 cup WHOLE PEANUTS
10 CARAMELS, melted

For the crust: In mixing bowl, combine crumbs, 3 Tbsp. chopped peanuts and margarine. Press on bottom and halfway up sides of 9-inch Springform pan; set aside. For the filling: In large mixing bowl, beat cream cheese with 1/3 cup brown sugar, corn syrup and corn starch. Add eggs, one at a time, beating well. Stir in 1/3 cup sour cream, vanilla, candy bars and remaining peanuts. Pour into prepared crust; bake at 350 degrees for 15 minutes. Reduce heat to 300, and bake 75 minutes, until top is not wet and glossy. Remove pan from oven, run knife around edge. Turn oven heat off; return pan to oven and let stand one hour. Remove from oven, cool and refrigerate overnight. For topping: Combine chocolate chips, remaining sour cream and remaining brown sugar. Remove cheese cake from refrigerator, remove pan edge and spread top with chocolate mixture. Sprinkle with whole peanuts, drizzle with melted caramels.

> *If you had to guess, where would you say you would find the only city in the nation that owns and operates its own railroad? Prineville uses its rail line to enhance its role as a lumbering and agricultural center.*

Carrot Cake Squares

1/3 cup MARGARINE
1/4 cup WATER
1 cup FLOUR
1 cup SUGAR
1/2 tsp. BAKING SODA
1/2 tsp. CINNAMON
1/2 tsp. NUTMEG

1/4 tsp. SALT
1 EGG, slightly beaten
1/4 cup BUTTERMILK
1/2 tsp. VANILLA
1 cup CARROTS, finely shredded
1/2 cup RAISINS
1/2 cup WALNUTS

In small saucepan, combine margarine and water. Bring to boil, stirring to melt margarine. Remove from heat and cool. In large bowl, stir together dry ingredients; add cooled margarine mixture, egg, buttermilk and vanilla. Stir until combined. Fold in carrots, raisins and walnuts; spread in 9 x 9 pan. Bake at 375 degrees, 25 to 30 minutes. For **frosting**: Mix **1/2 cup soft margarine, one cup sifted powdered sugar.** Beat together until well blended, add **1/4 tsp. orange peel** and **1 to 2 Tbsp. orange juice.**

Cocoa Apple Cake

1 cup MARGARINE
2 cups SUGAR
3 EGGS
2 1/2 cups FLOUR
2 Tbsp. COCOA
1 tsp. each BAKING SODA, CINNAMON, ALLSPICE
1 cup NUTS, finely chopped
1/2 cup CHOCOLATE CHIPS
1 Tbsp. VANILLA
2 cups APPLE, grated
1/2 cup WATER

Cream together margarine and sugar adding eggs one at a time, beating well. Combine dry ingredients and add to creamed mixture. Stir in remaining ingredients and pour into 9 x 13 greased pan. Bake at 350 degrees for 35 to 40 minutes.

Old Fashioned Raisin Bread Pudding

3 slices STALE BREAD, torn in small pieces
1/4 cup SUGAR
1/8 tsp. CINNAMON
1/8 tsp. SALT
1 1/2 cups MILK
2 EGGS, beaten
1 tsp. VANILLA
1/4 cup RAISINS
1/4 cup WALNUTS, coarsely chopped

Arrange bread pieces on bottom of buttered, deep casserole about 8 inches in diameter. In medium bowl, combine sugar, cinnamon and salt; add milk, eggs, vanilla and raisins. Mix well. Pour egg mixture evenly over bread, sprinkle with nuts. Bake at 350 degrees for 35 to 40 minutes, until knife in center comes out clean. Delicious topped with *'Best' Sauce* (below).

'Best' Sauce

1/2 cup POWDERED SUGAR
1/2 cup BUTTER, softened
1/2 cup WHIPPING CREAM

Beat powdered sugar with butter in a small saucepan, until smooth and creamy. Meanwhile beat whipping cream until stiff. Fold into sugar mixture. Heat, stirring occasionally until soft boil. Serve immediately. Makes 1 1/2 cups.

Note: Also very good, served on baked apples, apple dumplings, and steamed puddings. Apples bake quickly and easily in the microwave. Four apples take 5 to 6 minutes on high. Make a filling out of butter, brown sugar, cinnamon and nuts and place in cored apples before baking.

Angel Pie

4 EGGS, separated
1/4 tsp. CREAM OF TARTAR
1 1/2 cups SUGAR, divided
3 Tbsp. LEMON JUICE
2 tsp. GRATED LEMON RIND
1 cup WHIPPING CREAM, whipped

Beat egg whites until frothy. Add cream of tartar and gradually add 1 cup of sugar. Beat mixture until stiff and glossy. Bake in greased deep pie pan for 20 minutes at 275 degrees, and then 40 minutes at 300 degrees. Filling: Add 1/2 cup of sugar to beaten egg yolks. Mix in lemon juice and rind and cook in double boiler until thick. Add whipped cream and mix. When meringue shell has cooled, place filling on top. Refrigerate at least one hour. For best results, make pie in morning and keep cool until evening.

Brown Butter Butterscotch Pie

6 Tbsp. BUTTER, do not substitute
1 cup BROWN SUGAR, packed
1 cup BOILING WATER
3 Tbsp. CORN STARCH
2 Tbsp. FLOUR
1/2 tsp. SALT
1 2/3 cups MILK
3 EGG YOLKS, slightly beaten
1 tsp. VANILLA
1 (9 in. baked) PIE SHELL
WHIPPED CREAM

Melt butter in heavy skillet over low heat. When golden brown, add sugar; cook, stirring until mixture comes to boil. Stir in water, remove from heat. Mix corn starch, flour and salt in saucepan; blend in milk, stirring until smooth. Stir in sugar mixture, cook over medium heat, stirring until it comes to a boil. Boil one minute. Remove from heat, stir a little hot mixture into egg yolk, then blend into hot mixture. Cook one minute; add vanilla. Cool slightly, pour into pie shell. Chill and top with whipped cream.

Peanut Butter Pie

1 cup MILK
1 env. UNFLAVORED GELATIN
3/4 cup SUGAR, divided
4 EGGS, separated
1 tsp. VANILLA
1/2 cup PEANUT BUTTER
1/2 cup WHIPPING CREAM,
    whipped
1 (9 in. baked) PIE SHELL
1/2 cup HEAVY CREAM
4 oz. SEMI SWEET CHOCOLATE,
    cut in pieces
CHOPPED PEANUTS, for garnish

Pour milk in top of double boiler and heat over simmering water. Soften gelatin in milk; add 1/4 cup sugar, salt and egg yolks. Beat slightly to blend; cook, stirring constantly until mixture is thickened and it coats a metal spoon. Remove from heat; add vanilla and beat in peanut butter. Chill until thickened but not firm. Beat egg whites until foamy; gradually add remaining sugar, beating until stiff but not dry. Fold this meringue into peanut butter mixture, fold in whipped cream. Pile lightly in pie shell and chill until firm. To finish, combine heavy cream and chocolate in top of double boiler over simmering water. Cook, whisking constantly, until chocolate is melted and mixture is thick and creamy. Remove from heat, cool slightly, stirring occasionally. Spread over firm pie filling; sprinkle with chopped nuts. Allow to set before cutting pie.

Spectacular views are yours to enjoy at Ecola State Park, near Cannon Beach, which was named for a cannon which washed ashore from a shipwrecked schooner in 1846. It's the best place to see Tillamook Rock Lighthouse, a relic from the 1880's. Since being retired in 1957, it is today a columbarium.

Sour Cream Nugget Bars

Annette Wilkins — Sherwood

3 Tbsp. BUTTER
1/2 pkg. BETTY CROCKER® SOUR CREAM CHOCOLATE
    FUDGE CAKE MIX
1 1/2 cups MINIATURE MARSHMALLOWS
1 (6 oz. pkg.) CHOCOLATE CHIPS
1 (3 1/2 oz. can) COCONUT FLAKES
1 cup OREGON NUTS, any type, chopped
1 can SWEETENED CONDENSED MILK

Preheat oven to 350 degrees. In oven, melt butter in 9 x 13 pan, rotating until butter covers bottom. Sprinkle dry cake mix over butter. Then, sprinkle marshmallows, chocolate chips, coconut and nuts over dry cake mix. Pour milk evenly over top; bake about 30 minutes until golden brown. Run knife around edges to loosen; cut into bars when cool. Makes about 6 dozen, 1 1/2 inch bars.

Raspberry Pie Supreme

4 to 5 cups OREGON RASPBERRIES
1 (9 inch, unbaked) PIE SHELL
1 1/4 to 1 1/2 cups SUGAR
1 cup FLOUR
1/4 tsp. SALT
1 cup SOUR CREAM
2 tsp. SUGAR

Spread raspberries on bottom of pie shell; set aside. In mixing bowl, combine sugar, flour and salt. Stir in sour cream and mix well. Spoon this mixture over berries, spreading to edges of pie shell. Sprinkle with remaining sugar and bake at 450 degrees for 10 minutes. Reduce heat to 350, and bake another 30 minutes, or until top is lightly browned. Remove from oven and let cool before serving. Refrigerate leftovers.

Rhubarb Bars

Dorothy Markell — Portland

2 Tbsp. CORN STARCH
1/4 cup WATER
1 1/2 cups SUGAR
1 tsp. VANILLA
few drops RED FOOD COLORING
3 cups RHUBARB, cut up

Topping:
1 1/2 cups QUICK OATS
1 cup BROWN SUGAR
1 cup SHORTENING
1 1/2 cups FLOUR
1 tsp. BAKING SODA
1/2 cup NUTS, chopped, optional

Dissolve corn starch in water; add remaining ingredients and cook until thick. Cool and set aside. Meanwhile, mix all topping ingredients until crumbly. Place 3/4 of this mixture in a 9 x 13 pan. Pour cooled, cooked rhubarb mixture on top and cover with remainder of crumb mixture. Bake at 375 degrees for 30 to 35 minutes. Cut into squares when cooled.

Cake Mix Cookies

Annette Wilkins — Sherwood

1 pkg. CHOCOLATE CAKE MIX
1 EGG
3 Tbsp. WATER
1 (6 oz.pkg.) MINT CHOCOLATE CHIPS
1/2 cup NUTS, chopped

Combine ingredients, mixing well, chill. Spoon onto greased baking sheet, bake at 350 degrees about 10 to 12 minutes. Type of cake mix can be varied according to your tastes.

Bread Pudding

Lacey's Bomber Inn Restaurant — Milwaukie

2 1/4 loaves EGG BREAD, cut into 1/2 in. squares
1/3 cup MARGARINE, melted
2 1/4 cups BROWN SUGAR
3 Tbsp. CINNAMON
1 1/2 cups RAISINS
2 1/2 cups SUGAR
15 EGGS
1 lb. NON DAIRY CREAMER
12 cups WATER
1 Tbsp. VANILLA

Mix bread, margarine, brown sugar, cinnamon and raisins together. Separately, mix the sugar and eggs together; and the creamer and water together. Then, mix all wet ingredients together; add vanilla. Pour into bread mixture, mix. Spray a large deep pan with vegetable coating and pour in all ingredients. Bake 3 hours at 325 degrees uncovered. This recipe serves 32 people.

Mock Apple Pie

Ruth Christie — Baker City

3 EGG WHITES
1 cup SUGAR
1 tsp. VANILLA
20 RITZ® CRACKERS, crushed
1/2 cup OREGON NUTS, chopped
1 tsp. BAKING SODA

Beat egg whites and sugar until stiff; add vanilla. Combine cracker crumbs, nuts and baking soda; fold into egg mixture. Pour mixture into well greased pie pan. Bake at 350 degrees for 30 minutes. Top with whipped cream.

Index

Oregon Festivals & Celebrations

SPRING

Hood River Blossom Festival
Astoria-Warrenton Great Crab and Seafood Festival
Pendleton Underground "Comes Alive"
The Portland Cinco de Mayo Festival
Lincoln City Spring Kite Festival
Tygh Valley All-Indian Rodeo, The Dalles
Rhododendron Festival, Florence
Portland Rose Festival
Cannon Beach Sand Castle Contest
Cascade Festival of Music, Bend

SUMMER

The Britt Festival, Jacksonville
Oregon Bach Festival, Eugene
Waterfront Blues Festival, Portland
World Championship Timber Carnival, Albany
Oregon Trail Pageant, Oregon City
Oregon Coast Music Festival, Coos Bay
Lewis and Clark Historical Pageant, Seaside
Oregon Brewers Festival, Portland
International Pinot Noir Celebration,
    McMinnville
Mt. Hood Festival of Jazz, Gresham
The Bite: A Taste of Portland
Sunriver Music Festival
Oregon State Fair, Salem
Jedediah Smith Mountain Man Rendezvous
    and Buffalo BBQ, Grants Pass

FALL

Artquake, Portland
Pendleton Round-Up and Happy
    Canyon Pageant
Oktoberfest, Mt. Angel
Indian-Style Salmon Bake, Depoe Bay
Bandon Cranberry Festival
Eugene Celebration
Fall Festival, Corvallis
Indian Summer Folk Life Festival, St. Paul
Medford Jazz Jubilee
Hood River Harvest Festival

WINTER

Christmas at Pittock Mansion, Portland
Festival of Lights at The Grotto, Portland
Holiday Festival of Lights, Coos Bay/Charleston
Portland Parade of Christmas Ships
Whale of a Wine Festival, Gold Beach
Newport Seafood and Wine Festival

About the Author

As long as she can remember, it has been Janet Walker's passion to cook. She loves to experiment with new recipes and collect those of others.

A native of Tulsa, Oklahoma, her parents moved to the great Northwest when she was but eight years old. There she later met and married her husband, Ivan. They began their married life in an apartment in the Columbia River town of Astoria, over 45 years ago.

Janet now is a mother of three, and a grandmother to four. Her other interests include crocheting, playing bridge, and spending as much time as she can vacationing in her motorhome. In the summers, she spends her time preparing food for thousands of baseball fans, as the chief cook at a baseball park.

It is Janet's love for cooking that has prompted her to write her second cook book for Golden West Publishers. Her first book, **Washington Cook Book**, was published in 1994 and enjoys continued popularity.

The **Oregon Cook Book** features the delectable fruits, crunchy nuts, flavorful vegetables and juicy berries found here in the great state of Oregon. Janet has included, of course, many recipes for preparing the ocean seafoods garnered from our shimmering Pacific shores. Whether contributed, or from her own kitchen, these recipes will tantalize your taste buds.

Janet urges her readers to "add your own personal touches" to these recipes and advises, "Cooking need not be a chore, it should be fun! Especially if you let others help in the preparation. These recipes have been enjoyed in my kitchen, and they will be savored in yours, too!"

More Cook Books by Golden West Publishers

WASHINGTON COOK BOOK

This book captures the wonderful and tantalizing diversity of this scenic West Coast state. Over 185 recipes from Washington's dignitaries, fine restaurants, chefs (including Graham Kerr), cozy inns and homemakers. Entire section devoted to Northwestern seafood. This book includes trivia about the entire state, its festivals and landmarks. By Janet Walker.

5 1/2 x 8 1/2 — 128 Pages . . . $5.95

APPLE LOVERS COOK BOOK

Celebrating America's favorite—the apple! 150 recipes for main and side dishes, appetizers, salads, breads, muffins, cakes, pies, desserts, beverages and preserves, all kitchen-tested by Shirley Munson and Jo Nelson.

5 1/2 x 8 1/2 — 120 Pages . . . $6.95

CHRISTMAS IN WASHINGTON COOK BOOK

A sleigh full of Christmas traditions, festivals and treasured recipes from the Pacific Northwest. Many cooks, chefs, and innkeepers share their favorite holiday dishes including *Egg Nog Cranberry Salad, Moushella, Chicken & Herb Dumplings, Double Layered Pumpkin Pie* and more!

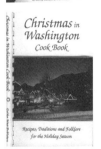

5 1/2 x 8 1/2—112 pages . . . $9.95

THE JOY OF MUFFINS
The International Muffin Cook Book

Recipes for German Streusel, Finnish Cranberry, Italian Amaretto, Greek Baklava, Chinese Almond, Jamaican Banana, Swiss Fondue, microwave section and ten recipes for oat bran muffins . . . 150 recipes in all! By Genevieve Farrow and Diane Dreher.

5 1/2 x 8 1/2 — 120 Pages . . . $5.95

SALSA LOVERS COOK BOOK

More than 180 taste-tempting recipes for salsas that will make every meal a special event! Salsas for salads, appetizers, main dishes and desserts! Put some salsa in your life! By Susan K. Bollin.

5 1/2 x 8 1/2 — 128 pages . . . $5.95

ORDER BLANK

GOLDEN WEST PUBLISHERS

☼ 4113 N. Longview Ave. • Phoenix, AZ 85014

602-265-4392 • **1-800-658-5830** • FAX 602-279-6901

Qty	Title	Price	Amount
	Apple Lovers Cook Book	6.95	
	Arizona Cook Book	5.95	
	Best Barbecue Recipes	5.95	
	Chili-Lovers Cook Book	5.95	
	Chip and Dip Lovers Cook Book	5.95	
	Christmas in Washington Cook Book	9.95	
	Citrus Lovers Cook Book	6.95	
	Cowboy Cartoon Cookbook	7.95	
	Easy RV Recipes	6.95	
	Easy Recipes for Wild Game & Fish	6.95	
	Joy of Muffins	5.95	
	Loaves of Fun	6.95	
	Oregon Cook Book	6.95	
	Pecan Lovers Cook Book	6.95	
	Quick-n-Easy Mexican Recipes	5.95	
	Recipes for a Healthy Lifestyle	6.95	
	Salsa Lovers Cook Book	5.95	
	Veggie Lovers Cook Book	6.95	
	Washington Cook Book	5.95	
	Wholly Frijoles! The Whole Bean Cook Book	6.95	

| Shipping & Handling Add ➠ | U.S. & Canada | $3.00 | |
| | Other countries | $5.00 | |

☐ My Check or Money Order Enclosed $

☐ MasterCard   ☐ VISA ($20 credit card minimum)

(Payable in U.S. funds)

Acct. No.   Exp. Date

Signature

Name   Telephone

Address

City/State/Zip

5/99   **Call for FREE catalog**   Oregon CB

This order form may be copied and faxed or mailed.